Summoned To Soar

The Five Stages of the Rise of a Woman

Angela Aja

SUMMONED TO SOAR: THE FIVE STAGES OF THE RISE OF A WOMAN

All scripture quotations, unless otherwise indicated, are taken from the New International Version (NIV) Holy Bible, New International Version®, NIV® Copyright ©1973, 1978, 1984, 2011 by Biblica, Inc.® Used by permission. All rights reserved worldwide. Scripture quotations marked (KJV) are from King James Version, Public Domain. Scripture quotations marked (MSG) are originally published by NavPress in English as THE MESSAGE: The Bible in Contemporary Language copyright 2002 by Eugene Peterson. All rights reserved. Scripture quotations marked (AMP) are from Amplified Bible, Copyright © 2015 by The Lockman Foundation, La Habra, CA 90631. All rights reserved. New King James Version(NKJV) Scripture taken from the New King James Version®. Copyright © 1982 by Thomas Nelson. Used by permission. All rights reserved. English Standard Version (ESV) The Holy Bible, English Standard Version. ESV® Text Edition: 2016. Copyright © 2001 by Crossway Bibles, a publishing ministry of Good News Publishers.

Copyright © 2018 by Angela Aja

Edited by: Lacie Hicks

For more information on this book and the author visit:
www.confidencebuildersinc.com

All rights reserved. This book or any portion thereofmay not be reproduced or used in any manner whatsoever
without the express written permission of the publisherexcept for the use of brief quotations in a book review.

Library of Congress Cataloging-in-Publication Data:
Aja, Angela
Summoned to Soar: The Five Stages of the Rise of a Woman / Angela Aja

First Edition, 2018

ISBN 978-1-7941-1593-4

Printed in the United States of America

Acknowledgements

The first acknowledgement I want to make is to my precious children, Jared, Ashley, Austin and Judson. You are the jewels in my crown. This book is for you. Your strength and resilience inspire me to rise a little higher every day and to answer the summons to soar. My prayer for each of you is that you go through the full process of development and emerge as the beautiful butterflies that you were created to be.

To my son-in law, Taylor and daughters-in-law, Alaona and Gabriella, you are the answer to my prayers – a gift to me. I love you for loving my children with such a deep love. Each of you have graced our family with a unique flair that makes us better together. Be fearless in your pursuit of your destinies.

To the little ones who light up my life in a way that is unexplainable, Roman, Finley, Havana and Jack, Mammaw loves you with a big love. May you go through the full process of your own development and rise to the highest heights.

To my parents and my sister who have stood by my side and supported me throughout the years emotionally, spiritually, physically, financially, and the list goes on... Where would I be without your love?

To the entire Charbonnet Family, who were instrumental as the silk lining of my cocoon, you surrounded me with grace as I was wrapped up in my cave of development.

To my dear friend, Ty Tillman, who said to me, "If you are going to trust the wind, then trust the wind." This dedication is scripted as a legacy to her son, Trace. Trace, may you trust the wind as you are summoned to soar.

To my butterfly sister, Janet Amador, who saw my butterfly long before I did. You spoke to my butterfly while I was in my cocoon which gave me the courage to stay in pursuit of the most authentic version of who I was created to be. I love you and appreciate your friendship.

All of my Girlfriends in God (GIGS) – words cannot express the love I have for you all for all of your love, prayers and encouragement; a group of spirit-led, supportive women who spoke to my butterfly even before my wings were fully developed.

Dr. Kathleen Bird, my first friend as a single woman, a caterpillar barely surviving in life. We have laughed together, cried together, grown together and transformed together. I love you and appreciate your friendship.

Lacie Hicks, the Editor and Publishing Manager of this book. You are the ying to my yang and the midwife to this baby. Thank you for your tireless collaboration, your commitment to living authentically and your love for apologetics. You were the perfect gift from God that enabled me to birth this message out of my heart and into print.

Finally, I would like to thank my heavenly Father, Jesus and the Holy Spirit for calling me to the Kingdom for such a time as this. I am grateful the synchronicities, breakthroughs and miracles that enabled me to endure the cocoon, breakout of the temporary confinement of my transformation and heed the summons to soar.

To sum it up in one sentence...I am grateful.

Table of Contents

A Note from the Author 1
Chapter 1 7
Chapter 2 22
Chapter 3 27
Phase One 39
Chapter 4 41
Chapter 5 50
Chapter 6 60
Phase Two 69
Chapter 7 71
Chapter 8 77
Chapter 9 85
Phase Three 91
Chapter 10 93
Chapter 11 109
Chapter 12 116
Phase Four 123
Chapter 13 125
Chapter 14 132
Chapter 15 139
Phase Five 151
Chapter 16 153
Chapter 17 164
Chapter 18 171
Conclusion 177
Chapter 19 179
Scriptural Basis for Coaching and Transformation 183
Notes 189
About the Author 194

A Note from the Author

As a transformational life coach, I have written this book in a way that provides an opportunity for personal development through the avenue of real-life stories and coaching principles with a scriptural foundation. In order to fully grasp the concepts contained in this book, the following is the basis for the groundwork from which this book was penned.

People ask me all of the time, "What is life coaching?"[1]

The word "coach" first appeared around 1830 and began being used in conjunction with sports. The word "coaching" was borrowed from the "coach" or "stagecoach" which was a vehicle of transportation to get you from where you are to where you want to be.

In the 1970s, Timothy Galloway wrote a book called *The Inner Game of Tennis*. The concept of the book was that the game of tennis could be mastered by focusing on your thoughts versus the physical game, itself. The book became a foundation for the development of coaching as we know it today, offering a new idea that success is more of an inner game than an outer game.

Coaching became an actual vocation in the 1990s.

The latest trend in business is that if you have had a breakthrough in some area, you become a "coach". I am thrilled that so many have the desire to help people shift but it's been my experience that "coaching" has become the new buzz word with a misunderstanding about what real coaching is. Many people who call themselves "coaches" today are actually "mentors."

True coaching comes from the perspective that:

- the answers are inside of you because you are the expert on you
- the answers are in the questions

As a Transformational Life Coach, I promote **authenticity** through observation, **analysis** through investigation and **action** through strategic planning. Coaching is an inward process by which the mind is renewed so that outward transformation can take place.

I call my specific brand of coaching, "Identity Coaching". My life long struggle with my identity has become specialization. This book is now a platform to present the lessons I have learned and the strategies I have employed to help women strengthen their inner foundation, re-styling their lives so that they radiate from the inside out and live with core confidence. The result of our time spent together will be clarity and confidence which will leave you feeling like you truly have command of your life.

What Coaching is NOT

Before you look at what coaching is, take a look at what coaching is not, according to International Coach Federation:

- **Therapy**: Therapy deals with healing pain, dysfunction, and conflict within an individual or in relationships. The focus is often on resolving difficulties arising from the past that hamper an individual's emotional functioning in the present, improving overall psychological functioning, and dealing with the present in more emotionally healthy ways. Coaching, on the other hand, supports personal and professional growth based on self-initiated change in pursuit of specific actionable outcomes. These outcomes are linked to personal or professional success. Coaching is future focused. While positive feelings/emotions may be a natural outcome of coaching, the primary focus is on creating actionable strategies for achieving specific goals in one's work or personal life. The emphases in a coaching relationship are on action, accountability, and follow through.

- **Consulting**: Individuals or organizations retain consultants for their expertise. While consulting approaches vary widely, the assumption is the consultant will diagnose problems and prescribe and, sometimes, implement solutions. With coaching, the assumption is that individuals or teams are capable of generating their own solutions, with the coach supplying supportive, discovery-based approaches and frameworks.

- **Mentoring**: A mentor is an expert who provides wisdom and guidance based on his or her own experience. Mentoring may include advising, counseling and coaching. The coaching process does not include advising or counseling and focuses instead on individuals or groups setting and reaching their own objectives.

- **Training**: Training programs are based on objectives set out by the trainer or instructor. Though objectives are clarified in the coaching process, they are set by the individual or team being coached, with guidance provided by the coach. Training also assumes a linear learning path that coincides with an established curriculum. Coaching is less linear without a set curriculum.

- **Athletic Development**: Though sports metaphors are often used, professional coaching is different from sports coaching. The athletic coach is often seen as an expert who guides and directs the behavior of individuals or teams based on his or her greater experience and knowledge. Professional coaches possess these qualities, but their experience and knowledge of the individual or team determines the direction. Additionally, professional coaching, unlike athletic development, does not focus on behaviors that are being executed poorly or incorrectly. Instead, the focus is on identifying opportunity for development based on individual strengths and capabilities.[2]

So, what is True Coaching?

Coaching is not my advice or my opinion but focuses on setting goals, creating outcomes and managing personal change.

Coaching is a collaborative partnership. Imagine a sacred space where you can feel heard, honored and valued; a safe, judgment-free zone to grow.

Coaching is a progressive, dynamic and thought-provoking conversation. It brings clarity to where you currently are, precision to where the dream of your heart longs to take you, what's standing in your way and builds a bridge between the gaps.

Coaching is about advancing your emotional intelligence, emotional responsibility, emotional resilience, and conscious awareness. It is present and future focused.

Coaching brings a person's potential and performance together to create results so that you can rock your life at a whole other level.

Coaching invites awareness and elicits client-generated solutions and outcomes.

Coaching comes from the perspective that you are a powerful chooser. It assumes that your current situation is the result of your mindset and that you chose your present mindset. The great news about this is that if you chose your current mindset but you do not like the results that you are getting then you can choose a new one.

Coaching delivers a chance to let go of old mental and emotional contracts that you have made with yourself and others and create new agreements. It challenges the old narrative that you have been telling yourself about the way things are so that you can re-script your story.

Coaching presents you with an opportunity to define whom you are by just *being* instead of *doing*. When you define who you are by what you do then you have to keep on doing it in order to prove who you are. However, if you discover who you are at your core, then what you do becomes a result of who you are. This mind-shift alone will release stress and cause major transformation. It is exhausting trying to prove who you are by what you do. That is what keeps you feeling like you are on the hamster wheel, unable to stop the cycle of a monotonous existence. Coaching is an invitation to be a "human being" vs. a "human doing". It is an opportunity to let go of who you "should" be and discover who you ARE at your core. Coaching presumes that you were created for more than an ordinary existence. Coaching helps you discover the extraordinary life of impact that you were created for.

Your next level will always become your ceiling. Where you are now was once something you were attaining to achieve. What you have currently been able to achieve will, at some point, become the ceiling that keeps you stuck where you are. By up-leveling your mindsets, you will be able to "raise the roof" on your self-belief ceiling and step up into your next level. It all begins with your mindsets.

Throughout the pages of this book, I will introduce you to concepts that will shift your mindset from surviving to thriving. I will walk you through a process of getting clear about where you currently are, where you really want to go and what is standing in your way so that you can live a life of significance, fulfillment and true joy.

Chapter 1

Rise Up and Snap Back

"Rise up, my love, my fair one, and come away." Song of Solomon 2:10

There's just something about a woman who is committed to rise. A woman on the rise is:

Resilient – A woman on the rise is resilient. If you are resilient you have come through some stuff; you have experienced life. Deep down inside, a resilient woman knows that her setbacks prepare her for her comeback. If you are resilient, you know who you are – you are strong, you have tenacity; you have natural buoyancy that gives you the ability to snap back. Something in your gut tells you that where you are in your journey is not your final destination. You are compelled to overcome obstacles and breakthrough barriers which try to limit you to a life of ordinary.

Intentional – A woman on the rise is intentional. If you are intentional, you are deliberate and focused, committed to the full process of development in order to step into your call. A tug of war between your destiny and your day to day grind will always entice you to succumb to the disruption of the pointless obligations – but you are a woman on the rise – intentional about your focus and the direction you move in.

Spirit-led – A woman on the rise is Spirit-led. If you are a Spirit-led woman you do not lean on your own understanding in your decision-making process. You are Kingdom-minded with eternal values and priorities. You are perceptive, guided by your intuition and you have learned to trust yourself. You are not daunted by what you see, and you exhibit faith in the unseen. As a Spirit-led woman, you do not always follow conventional wisdom. You are not influenced by the approval or the dissatisfaction of others. A woman on the rise is a Spirit-led woman who is committed to a vision that encompasses a vastness that extends far beyond her own individual life.

Empowered – A woman on the rise is empowered. As a woman on the rise, you know that you are empowered for the job. You are not afraid of your personal power. You have a revelation that the acknowledgment of your personal power does not detract from the power of God; rather it is an outward expression of the power of God that resides inside of you. As an empowered woman, you use your power to influence your own past, present, and future. You influence your own thoughts, patterns, and behaviors so that the influence you have over your own life begins to exude out of you and impact those within your sphere of influence. As a woman on the rise, you are empowered from within.

In the pages of this book, you will be inspired to be resilient, be intentional, be Spirit-led and to live empowered as you rise up, step into your call and make the impact that you were placed on this earth to make.

The Five Phases

There are five phases that every woman has the opportunity to walk through. One phase builds upon the next phase, each one preparing you to step into your highest call – your divine purpose. There is nothing more fulfilling than knowing who you are, why you are here and what you are here to do. But it is too easy to get stuck in one phase or another and never progressing to the final phase – *The Rise*.

The first phase begins with a conventional life – *The Ordinary*. In the middle of *The Ordinary*, life is normal. Faith for the mundane prods you along as you go through the motions of day to day living. You learn and grow, taking in life as it comes along. Fairy tales speak to the seeds of greatness and whisper to the princess within. Seeds of a dream of queenly impact are deposited within your heart. This phase mimics the life of a slow-moving caterpillar.

Somewhere in the middle of *The Ordinary*, a setback occurs, many times in the form of a crisis. This setback thrusts you into the second phase – *The Cave*. *The Cave* is often a dark, lonely time of life that can either be the death of you, internally or the place where transformation can take place. *The Cave* is where you decide to relinquish control, let patience have her way with you so that transformation can take place. *The Cave* mimics the cocoon where a caterpillar goes through the process of metamorphosis and turns into a butterfly.

In *The Cave*, the third phase begins to unfold – *The Becoming*. *The Becoming* is the metamorphosis that takes place inside of the cocoon. The metamorphosis is the transformation that a woman goes through as she lets go of the woman who was fashioned by fears, insecurities and self-imposed limitations. It is in this phase that she begins to awaken to her authenticity and come into alignment with her divine assignment.

Once the transformation has occurred, the fourth phase begins – *The Debut*. This is a season of breakthrough. Just as a butterfly, once fully formed, breaks out of the cocoon, a woman in *The Debut* phase of life has stepped into the most authentic version of whom she was created to be. She knows her mission, vision, and purpose and she is ready to be seen and heard. This newly fashioned woman is ready to use her new wings to fly higher and further than ever before.

All four of the first phases culminate in the fifth and final stage which is *The Rise*. *The Rise* is where you begin to live the life of influence and impact that you were being prepared for.

Each phase of advancement follows the same pattern of development as that of the transformation of a caterpillar into a butterfly. From the heroes of faith to the champions of old, these same five phases can be seen in the lives of anyone who has ever been a world-changer or history maker. Transitioning in and out of each phase requires being comfortable with the unknown and not being afraid of risk. Learning to transition with grace and ease will allow you to surrender to the process of development that is summoning you to soar to the heights that you were born to dance in.

It is when you get stuck in one phase or the other that suffering occurs. (When I say suffering, I mean fear, frustration, self-sabotage, overwhelm, underwhelm, exhaustion...) Each phase comes with a set of tests and trails that are necessary for graduation. Only when you become dissatisfied with *The Ordinary*, will you submit to *The Cave*. The degree to which you embrace your time in *The Cave* will directly affect how much you "become." Your ability to yield to the process of *The Becoming* affects your ability to step into *The Debut*. Finally, you can only rise to the degree that you have surrendered to the season of The Debut. The graduation of each phase directly impacts your ability to RISE.

Going through the full process of all of the phases is of utmost importance if you are to advance to *The Rise*. The Rise is the ultimate destination of every woman and is God's desire for her. There is no need to ask if *The Rise* is God's will for your life. His heart is for you to step into your queenly anointing that He predestined for you. It is His will for you to step into the call that He placed inside of you from before your foundations. He sees you in your completed state and He is calling you to rise up. He is calling you to step into your call so that you can assist Him in establishing His kingdom and creating heaven on earth.

When Life Doesn't Turn Out as Expected

> *"We must be willing to let go of the life we planned so as to have the life that is waiting for us." – Joseph Campbell*

If life has not gone as expected then you are perfectly positioned to RISE.

As a little girl, you dream of the perfect life. You carefully construct the life of your dreams in your imagination – but something happens along the way...

- You realize your Prince Charming is really a frog
- Your castle is more like a grass hut
- Your precious angel children morph into unrecognizable beings
- Sickness and disease come and rob you of a life of "normal"
- Your money gets up and walks away as if it had legs
- You end up in a job that feels more like a prison
- You fail at something you just knew you could succeed at

- You lose loved ones that you thought would always be by your side
- You suffer betrayal, loss, and devastation

AND THEN YOU HAVE A SET-BACK!

A setback is any obstacle that impedes you from moving forward. A setback can leave you feeling disenchanted and disillusioned. A setback brings you to a fork in the road and is often accompanied by lack of clarity, survival mechanisms, and disappointment. Disappointment can be a natural response to any kind of setback whether big or small. If disappointment is not addressed then it will turn into underwhelm – a deep disappointment and regret about the way things *should* have been.

In order to cope with the disappointments and disenchantments of life, you thrust yourself into a cycle that I call the "Deadly D Cycle" – also known as UNDERWHELM. This cycle starts with a deep sense of ***disappointment*** about the way things were supposed to turn out. Then, in order to survive, you push all of those feelings down with ***denial***. You have so many plates to keep spinning that it is easier to deny your own sense of disappointment and forge ahead with ***distractions***. You keep yourself distracted by ***doing, doing, doing*** instead of being. The problem is that when you lay your head on the pillow at night and all you are left with is your thoughts, you feel like a ***diminished*** version of yourself. You feel ***drained*** and ***depleted*** because you give and give and give while neglecting yourself which leads back to the beginning of the cycle of feeling a deep sense of disappointment.

The root of disappointment lies within our expectations. It is all about our expectations. An expectation is an assumption or a presumption. An expectation is not reality. It is nothing more than a theory or a hypothesis. It is the result of a fairytale about the way things should be that that has been concocted in your mind.

But what if life not going as planned was all a part of the plan?

Underwhelm, a deep disappointment about the way things have turned out, is directly related to the expectations that we have established about life and the people that we do life with. The problem with expectations is that they become a heavy burden to bear. When you presume them on your relationships, you may be the only one with the expectation, so it sets the other person up for failure. Your expectations are too heavy of a load to put on yourself or someone else to carry and they may not be equipped to live up to that expectation.

Dropping expectations about the way life was supposed to turn out will bring a whole new level of peace of mind and it will open up space in your mind for creativity to be able to construct a life that you love. Take the pressure off of yourself and others and enjoy the life you have in front of you.

Throughout this book, I am going to give you the tools that you need to lay down the heavy burden of expectations and STOP "underwhelm" from eating your lunch, stealing your joy and keeping you from a life of purpose! You can break out of the cycle! It is DOABLE! You can RISE UP and live a life of significance, fulfillment and true joy even if your circumstances do not change. Your setbacks have set you up for a comeback. I am going to show you how!

Lessons from a Rubber-band

Setbacks show up in your life to give you an opportunity to snap-back. Expectations and disappointment can stretch you to the breaking point. Have you ever felt like a rubber-band that is being stretched way beyond its capacity to stretch? Women on the rise know how to be resilient and snap-back from a setback.

Mother Teresa said, "I know God won't give me anything I can't handle. I just wish He didn't trust me so much."

I can relate to this statement way too much! I have endured things that I never dreamed that I would experience and in the middle of those times of crisis, I felt like a rubber-band that was literally about to bust. In those moments, I have wondered how I will keep it all together. How can I stretch any further? How can I keep going without SNAPPING?

Resilience is the ability to snap-back after compression or being stretched beyond one's normal capacity. The art of resilience is not for surviving, but for thriving. Resilience is not enduring. Resilience is what happens after you have endured; it is the flourishing that begins to happen after you have undergone the push and the pull of being extended past your limitations.

Resilience has to do with the expansion of your capacity. Capacity is the innate potential for growth, personal development, and accomplishment.

Capacity is increased by expansion and expansion is impossible without the stretching. To stretch is to extend, spread out or to lengthen. Being stretched requires elasticity. Elasticity is a response to change. You will never know how resilient you are until your elasticity is challenged and you are stretched beyond your capability. Your response to change reveals your capacity. The greater your capacity is, the more resilient you can be.

Resilience is absolutely necessary in order for the comeback to take place. Resilience is the difference between staying stuck in disappointment and moving forward. It is not what happens to you that causes your suffering; it is your response to what has happened. Resilience is your new response. Many of my clients are able to tap into their resilience after doing the work that comes with coaching. One such client suffered severely from postpartum depression that left her feeling stuck in guilt and shame. After several sessions, she began to respond to the emotional triggers that kept her in a cycle of spinning her wheels rather than reacting to her feelings of negativity. She responded with resilience and now works with women who suffer from the same symptoms. She allowed her circumstances to stretch her and enlarge her capacity for a greater impact.

Rubber-band Takeaways

There are three takeaways from the rubber-band that you can incorporate into your life to inspire resilience. First, rubber bands are made of polymers. Polymers are chains of molecules which are cross-linked to provide a network. The cross-links determine the properties of the rubber band. In other words, whom you are connected to really does make a difference. Cross-links provide memory. Connect with people who remind you can stretch farther than you think you can. Be intentional as you rely on your network to help you stretch further.

Weekend Baptism

Down at the lake, out on the dock, I stood there looking into the murky lake water, shaking with fear, trying not to hyperventilate as I thought about what I was getting ready to do. With my network of encouragers by my side, one friend was in the water, treading patiently and another friend holding my hand, the girls waited for me to take the plunge that I had been avoiding for many years. A few months ago, in a group coaching session, my dear friend and life coach, Elizabeth, had asked a few of us what our deepest fear was. I had been fearless throughout my life when it comes to making bold moves, but there was no hesitation when my pen hit the paper in full disclosure of what my biggest fear was. As we went around the group, one by one, sharing our deepest fear, I listened as the others seemed so much more meaningful than mine. Before I knew it, my turn was at hand and I sheepishly eked out, "I am afraid of deep water." I could almost hear the giggles. Elizabeth inquired about this fear. "What about it, are you afraid of?" The words came spilling out of my mouth before I could catch them. I answered boldly, "Because I am afraid of what is under there that I cannot see." She smiled and lovingly said, "I wonder if that is a metaphor for your life." Ugh...those words went straight through me like an arrow hitting the bullseye.

Yes, it had indeed been a metaphor for my life. At that moment, I realized that there were things I had been avoiding because I was afraid of what was lying underneath, in the dark murky waters of my soul. I was afraid of what I could not see. Since I couldn't see it, maybe if I just ignored it, it would just go away. But ignoring those issues was not serving anyone. I went home that night and made a list of all of those little nagging conversations I had been avoiding, all of the activities that I had been sidestepping for fear that there would be more to the story and all of the people that I been dodging for fear that a confrontation would stir up more trouble. At the end of our weekend, I made a bold proclamation that the next time I was around lake water that I jump right in. Once I got home, with fearless abandon, I began taking action; jumping in the lake, so to speak, crossing things off of my list and feeling the freedom that comes with conquering your fears. But there was still one thing that needed to be done...actually jumping in the lake.

A few months later, the girls and I gathered for a reunion that took place at...you guessed it...a house on the lake. Wow, how convenient for me (knees knocking, hands shaking and heart pounding out of my chest.) Yes, this was my day. As we assembled, one by one, we went around the room, catching up since the last time we had been together. Of course, they all remembered that I had professed my freedom from my fear of deep water and had committed to jumping in. In preparation for my big plunge, we talked about my fear and how it related to my life as a whole. One of the girls related my jumping in the lake to a baptism. At that moment, something jumped inside of me. Suddenly, I had a new revelation of what jumping in the lake would mean to me. My network was causing me to stretch further than I could have gone on my own. With everyone's assistance, I started making a list of all of the things I would leave in the lake: unfounded fears, self-limiting beliefs, and mindsets that were keeping me stuck. Then, I made a list of what I was coming out of the lake with: fearlessness, freedom, focus and listening to the feedback that life was giving me, rather than creating a fantasy. So, before the day had ended, I found myself standing on the edge of the dock, right where my story began.

One...two...three...PLUNGE! I did it! I jumped in the lake! I jumped into the dark, murky water and nothing came up from below and dragged me under. I jumped in the crisp, cool water and it refreshed me. The water caressed my skin and comforted me. All of that time that I had spent being afraid of the deep, I had been missing out on a blessing.

Somewhere along the line, I developed a gripping fear of deep water or any water that I could not see through. But as it relates to being a metaphor for life, I was choosing not to jump into the parts of my life where I feared there was more lurking beneath the surface. Yes, you may have to investigate what lies beneath when you go into the cocoon. Yes, you might stir up the dark, murky waters of your soul and come face to face with the things you have been avoiding but when you do, nothing will reach and drag you under. What I learned is, if you rely on your network, you can stretch further and dive deeper...and that was my weekend baptism.

The Art of the Snap-back

Second, becoming more pliable will give you the ability to snap back instead of snap. The thermodynamics of a rubber band's elasticity causes it to react differently than most materials when heat is applied. Heat makes a rubber band brittle and breakable. Flexibility – giving up the need to control the outcome will give you the ability to snap-back instead of snap when life turns up the heat.

I remember reading the following story of a young woman.

A young woman went to her mother and told her about her life and how things were so hard for her. She did not know how she was going to make it and wanted to give up. She was tired of fighting and struggling. It seemed as one problem was solved, a new one arose.

Her mother took her to the kitchen. She filled three pots with water and placed each on a high fire. Soon the pots came to boil. In the first she placed carrots, in the second she placed eggs, and in the last, she placed ground coffee beans. She let them sit and boil, without saying a word.

In about twenty minutes she turned off the burners. She fished the carrots out and placed them in a bowl. She pulled the eggs out and placed them in a bowl. Then she ladled the coffee out and placed it in a bowl. Turning to her daughter, she asked, "Tell me, what do you see?" "Carrots, eggs, and coffee," she replied.

Her mother brought her closer and asked her to feel the carrots. She did and noted that they were soft. The mother then asked the daughter to take an egg and break it. After pulling off the shell, she observed the hard-boiled egg. Finally, the mother asked the daughter to sip the coffee. The daughter smiled as she tasted its rich aroma. The daughter then asked, "What does it mean, mother?"

Her mother explained that each of these objects had faced the same adversity – boiling water. Each reacted differently. The carrot went in strong, hard, and unrelenting. However, after being subjected to the boiling water, it softened and became weak. The egg had been fragile. Its thin outer shell had protected its liquid interior, but after sitting through the boiling water, its inside became hardened. The ground coffee beans were unique, however. After they were in the boiling water, they had changed the water.

"Which are you?" she asked her daughter. "When adversity knocks on your door, how do you respond? Are you a carrot, an egg or a coffee bean?"

Are you the carrot that seems strong, but with pain and adversity wilts, becomes soft, and loses strength? Are you the egg that starts with a malleable heart, but changes with the heat? Does your shell look the same, but on the inside are you bitter and tough with a stiff spirit and hardened heart?

Or are you the coffee bean? Actually, changing the hot water, the very circumstance that brings the pain. When the water gets hot, it releases the fragrance and flavor. If you are like the bean, when things are at their worst, you get better and change the situation around you. Act like a rubber band and allow the heat of life to bring out your flexibility so that your fragrance and flavor can be released for greater impact.

STRETCHHHHH

Third, the rubber band was created to stretch. When life stretches you to the point that you feel like you are about to break, it is not because you have done something wrong. Life is not against you. God allows the stretching because He created you with the capacity to make a bigger impact. When the networks of molecules inside of a rubber band are stretched, entropic force takes over. Entropy is the tendency for all matter to evolve toward a state of uniformity. There will always be forces at work trying to get you to snap-back from the stretching, only to go back to the way things were. The stretching brings you out of your comfort zone and snaps you back to a place that reminds you of your original, authentic design – that for which you were originally created to be. You were created to be stretched.

Getting comfortable with being uncomfortable will keep entropic forces from coaxing you back into a state of uniformity. You were created for more than a homogenous life of barely getting by. In December of 1920, Amelia Earhart paid to go on her first plane ride. While it only lasted ten minutes it changed her life forever. Few women were involved in the aviation field at that time. While her gusty determination is attributed for her success, it is believed that it was her confidence – her willingness to go after the impossible and her belief in herself that she could accomplish it, is what got the job done. Amelia Earhart chose not to conform to previously set standards. Instead, she located her impossible and went after it.

A rubber band can be stretched twice its size and still return to its original shape. You were designed to expand past your natural state. The point is you can handle more than you think you can. You are resilient!

I am putting out a clarion call to women who are ready to lay aside disappointment and to be resilient as you snap-back so that you can come back after a setback and RISE UP!

Chapter 2

The Power of Transformation

"The essence of transformation stirs hope through the pain, faith for the mundane and leaves within you a gut feeling that none of it is vain." Angela Aja

Transformation is an integral part of the journey of a woman who is being summoned to soar. What is transformation? Webster's Dictionary says, "To transform is to change markedly, the appearance or form of. It is to change in composition or structure."[3] Transformation is a mindset shift that causes a change in your thoughts, patterns, and behaviors. Transformation shifts your thoughts from *what you do* to *who you are.* The act of transforming is to redefine, redesign, refashion, revise, revamp, to adjust or to alter; it is to go through a metamorphosis. Just as metamorphosis is the process by which a caterpillar transforms into a butterfly, transformation is the metamorphosis that a woman goes through that awakens her to her authentic design, brings her into alignment with her divine assignment and authorizes her for a life of impact.

There are two types of metamorphoses that take place in the insect kingdom. The first type is called "incomplete metamorphosis." This is where the young look like the adults but without wings. For example, baby grasshoppers, crickets and dragonflies bear a resemblance to their adult counterpart, but without having their wings developed. The second type is called "complete metamorphosis." In this occurrence, the young look nothing like the adults. They do not eat the same food and their mode of transportation is completely different. In the case of the butterfly, it goes through complete transformation; a complete change in structure and composition. 4 In the case of a woman on the journey toward *The Rise*, her expedition leads to a complete metamorphosis in which her life is transfigured from one way of being to another – a true, complete transformation.

> *Romans 12:2 says, "Do not conform to the pattern of this world, but be transformed by the renewing of your mind. Then you will be able to test and approve what God's will is--his good, pleasing and perfect will." NIV*

The process of renewing your mind results in a true transformation that takes place between your ears – in your mind – your thoughts, patterns, and beliefs. Transformation begins in your thoughts, which then affects your patterns and behaviors causing your outer world to shift and align with your inner world. As your thinking changes, your circumstances change.

The Essence of Transformation

The essence of transformation stirs hope through the pain, faith for the mundane and leaves within you a gut feeling that none of it is in vain. The essence of a thing is the fundamental ingredient that sets it apart. The essence of transformation is that it is a key component at the heart of change that determines the outcome of a setback. At the heart of transformation is an essence; a feeling of hope that comes from a knowing in the depth of your being that no matter what you are presently going through or what you have gone through in your past, there has been a purpose for it and it is bringing out the best in you.

A woman on her journey toward *The Rise* may have experienced a setback or two but she possesses *the essence of transformation*. This essence of transformation is what makes her resilient and strong; it prepares her for her comeback.

At Some Point, You've Got to Cross Over Into Your 41st Year

"At some point, you've got to cross over into your 41st year! It's time to cross over into your promise land!" I was fired up and preaching good! The "Amen's!" were strong that day. I was preaching at our church in Austin. I was forty years old and co-pastoring alongside my husband at the time. I was preaching about how the children of Israel wandered for forty years in the desert before they crossed over into the Promised Land. I had heard many good sermons about wandering for forty years in the desert, but I had never heard anyone preach about the *41st year*. It occurred to me one day, that at the end of the 40th year, the children of Israel exited the desert and entered the promised land going into their *41st year*. I was on the cusp of turning 41 and I knew that I was headed straight for my promised land. Looking back, I am not exactly sure what I was expecting my promised land to look like, but somehow, I knew things would be different once I had "crossed over."

I have always loved cooking and I was raised to be a "foodie" even before it was cool to be a "foodie." Something was stirring inside of me. Raising four kids had been a full-time job. All of the kids were in school and I was ready to venture out and do something for myself; something that I was passionate about. One day, I journeyed out to visit a few of the local cooking schools. When I entered through the doors of Le Cordon Bleu Texas Culinary Academy, it was as if I was walking through the pearly gates. I could hear the angels singing as I crossed the threshold. I had just entered "foodie heaven." My heart was pounding with excitement as I walked down the hall and saw all of the students and instructors dressed in chef coats and chef hats. The sweet and savory aromas that filled the air triggered my saliva glands as if I was Pavlov's dog, and my mouth watered uncontrollably. I had found my tribe, my people; I was home.

I sat down with the registrar. I knew that this was what I wanted to do, but this was the first time I would be doing something for myself. So many questions were flooding my mind. Could I handle this? Was I strong enough and smart enough to do this? It would require sacrifice from the whole family. Would they be willing to sacrifice for me? Would they resent me for doing something for myself? Finally, I quieted my mind down and started asking the questions that really mattered. As I inquired about the starting date, what I heard next blew my mind. The registrar responded, "The next class begins on August 19th." That was my 41st birthday! Just like the children of Israel wandered for 40 years and then crossed over into the promised land on the first day of their *41st year*, I was done wandering and I was ready to cross over into my promised land of purpose on the first day of my *41st year.*

Little did I know that crossing into my promised land became the birthplace of my transformation. That season marked an awakening inside of me that changed me forever. I had been wandering for 40 years, questioning who I was and what I was here to do but the first day of my *41st year* catapulted me into a transformative process that rocked me at my core.

Life was about to throw me a curve ball that I had not seen coming but I had *the essence of transformation* and I trusted this to be true:

> *Romans 8:28 "And we know that all things work together for good to them that love God, to them who are the called according to his purpose." KJV*

Chapter 3

The Power of Transition

*"When shifts and transitions in life shake you to the core, see that as a sign of
greatness that's about to occur."* Chelsea Dinen

A transition is the passageway that ushers an individual from one phase of development to another – from one season to the next. Transition creates an ebb and flow between your stages of development. It is absolutely necessary to understand the evolutionary principles of transition so that you can flow from one phase to another with grace and ease. Transitioning between the phases will keep you from getting stuck and spinning your wheels and it will move you forward faster.

As a woman, transition is something that your body does instinctively. You naturally shift from childhood to adolescence, to womanhood and then finally to menopause. In childbirth, your body transitions from labor to the opening of the womb so that you can deliver your baby. Muscles contract and relax to expand the birthing canal, preparing your body for transition – the transition that reveals what was once hidden in the womb to the life you now embrace in your arms. Your body runs its natural course intuitively without your spoken direction. However, your mind does not always cooperate with life's transitions as spontaneously as your body does.

As a mother of four, I am well acquainted with transition. I remember the transition of going from labor to pushing. With my first born, I laid on my back in bed all through labor so my body was not working in conjunction with gravity, which made the whole process take longer. When they put me on the table and started to wheel me down the hall into the delivery room, I remember looking up at the doctor and saying, "I DON'T WANT TO DO THIS...I CHANGED MY MIND!" But there was no turning back! By the time I had my fourth child, I was no longer a novice at giving birth. I positioned myself in a way that my body would work with the natural elements of gravity and my delivery time was cut down to a third of the time.

I remember when my daughter went into the hospital to have her first baby. Everything was going great. She was actually ahead of schedule and her body was responding exactly as it was supposed to. As the nurse did her routine check, she was shocked to find that my daughter was already dilated and ready to push. They scurried everyone out of the delivery room and called the doctor. We took our seats in the waiting room. Every time someone walked through the doors, we nearly jumped out of our seats, ready to make a mad dash to the delivery room to meet my sweet little granddaughter.

As we waited, the seconds seemed like minutes and the minutes seemed like hours. "Why was it taking so long?" we thought to ourselves. They should have called us into the room to meet our granddaughter by now! We could not take the suspense any longer. We sneaked down the hall, tiptoed up to the delivery room and pressed our ears against the door to try and hear what was taking so long. As we stood outside the door, we could hear the doctor telling Ashley to push. One of the nurses stepped outside of the room and we practically tackled her to give us more information. We bombarded her with questions. "What is going on?" "Is everything ok?" "Why is it taking so long?" "How much longer will it be?" She was stuck in transition.

I remember feeling an overwhelming rush of discouragement wash over me. I wanted to run in and shove the doctor out of the way and take over the situation. I felt helpless. I felt anxious. One minute, thoughts of fear and dread were racing through my mind. The next minute, I felt hopeful and full of faith. Then the fear would raise its ugly head again. All I could do was pray and wait.

I think the worst part of transition is the feeling of a lack of control. Even if everything seems to be lining up perfectly, that does not guarantee when or how the outcome will take place. I remember living in Chicago most of my life and the transitions between seasons were always unpredictable. I would leave my house in the morning, all bundled up in my fall fashion only to have to un-layer throughout the day down to my summer-time attire. You could turn the heat on in the morning and the air conditioner on in the afternoon. The calendar said that the season was fall but the atmosphere still said summer. There was no amount of control that could be exerted over the weather. The weather does what the weather wants to do, but eventually, the weather lines up with the calendar.

Have you ever been stuck in transition; stuck in between seasons? Have you ever been waiting with anticipation for the cool, refreshing winds of your next season, but the sun is still bearing down? If it is still hot out, then the season has not changed, no matter what the calendar says! You can quote T.D. Jakes, "Get ready, get ready, get ready, get ready!!!," and sing, "He's an on-time God!" until you are blue in the face, but that next season will show up at exactly the right time and exactly the right way.

I know what it feels like to carry a vision as if I was carrying a baby in my womb. I know what it is like to carry a dream in my heart for what seems like nine long months and to be ready to transition and give birth to that vision NOW! I know what it is like to have carried the next phase of my destiny around to full term, nurtured it, cared for it and protected it from naysayers and even from my own negative thoughts. I know what it is like to have expanded in ways that I did not even know were possible and feel like I should be holding this thing in my arms right now and experiencing all of the joy that is going to accompany my next level. But it is still in the birthing canal; stuck in transition. I know how it feels to push and push and push to birth the next level out now because you are ready now. Sometimes though, your next level is so immense that it needs to be birthed at the perfect time, with the right support system around you and when you are properly positioned.

If you misappropriate where you are in the process of transition then there is a danger of judging the matter and making counteractive decisions that keep you stuck in transition.

Wandering and Wondering

Take, for example, the children of Israel in the Bible. They were given an opportunity to exit the place that had held them captive for generations. They had escaped from the oppressive season of *The Cave* but they griped and complained, wanting to go back to their previous phase of development to which they had grown accustomed. They had an opportunity to enter into their promised land, but rather than transition with grace and ease, they misappropriated their season of transition and they stayed stuck in their wandering and wondering for way longer than they needed to

– 40 years longer. They were only a few days away from their promised land the whole time.

Life is cyclical by nature and you do not get a hall pass to exit one phase of development until you are fully equipped and ready to step into your next phase of development, abundantly prepared. In other words, you will get a chance to go around that mountain again. Allowing transition to accomplish its purpose in you will make your journey easier, more enjoyable and more effective.

Transition will show up differently throughout your phases of development. Searching for more may beckon you to transition from one phase or another. A setback in the form of a crisis might coerce you out of one phase and into the next. Self-examination may guide you from where you are to where you want to be. A struggle has the ability to shift you in and out of phases. No matter how transition reveals itself, surrender to the process of change. Go through the full evolution that is beckoning you to a higher place.

To transition is to make a change-over, a shift or go through an evolution. Transition happens backward so it can leave you feeling insecure and unstable if you are not keenly aware of what is happening. Transition happens in three stages. Let's take a look at the three stages of transition: an ending, the neutral zone, and a new beginning.[5]

Transition Begins with an Ending

Transition begins with an ending. When one phase of development comes to an end and you stand in the doorway of your next season, you have to be ready to step out of the old and into the new. Transition lays the framework for the crossover from one season to the next. You may notice abrupt endings such as losing a job or a relationship that suddenly changes. If you do not understand transition, you may see these happenings as "life is falling apart" or "God must be mad at me – what am I doing wrong?" However, if you are aware that you are in transition, you can confidently exit one phase of development and enter into your new season with grace and ease.

Emotions that are often associated with the beginning of transition are fear, shock, blame, shame or guilt. The strategic action is to simply let go and let transition do her thing. Growing up as a preacher's kid, my dad would always end his sermons with a story. One such story was about a little boy. He climbed up on the counter while his mom was preoccupied with the laundry. He plunged his hand into the cookie jar but he had filled his hands with so many cookies that he could not pull his hand out of the cookie jar. His mother came in and caught him red-handed before he could get any out. The moral of the story is that sometimes you just have to let go of some things so that you can enjoy the sweetness that is available to you. If he had let go of the handful of the cookies and just taken one, then he could have pulled his hand out of the cookie jar and eaten the cookie.

If abrupt endings are showing up in your life, do not freak out! Let go of the last season so you can enjoy the sweetness of the new season that is right around the corner. Consider the fact that you may have stepped into the beginning stages of a transition.

The Neutral Zone

The Neutral Zone finds you smack dab in the middle of a transition. Once the previous season has ended and you are heading into your next season, you will find yourself in *The Neutral Zone* which feels like the abyss of the unknown. Take a deep breath! You will not be there forever. You will know you are in *The Neutral Zone* when things have ended but the new beginning has not arrived yet.

The Neutral Zone can feel like one of the most frustrating parts of transition to be in.

Emotions associated with *The Neutral Zone* are anxiety, uncertainty or even confusion. You know in your "knower" that you have graduated from one phase of development but you also know that you have not stepped into your next season yet. You can "name it and claim it" or try to "blab it and grab it," but your next season is like the wind. It cannot be captured and ordered around. Like the changing seasons of the weather, the calendar may say "spring" but spring ain't sprung until the flowers bloom.

If you feel like you are in the "no-mans-land" of seasons then you are probably right on target. You are in *The Neutral Zone* of transition. And guess what that means? Your new beginning is right around the corner.

New Beginnings

Transition always ends with a new beginning. New beginnings can be so exciting. They can be filled with wonder and awe. However, new beginnings can also bring up new insecurities. You have never been here before, so along with the excitement, frustration of learning new ways of being in your new season can show up. Do not become so enamored with the new beginning that you get stuck there.

Integrate all of the lessons from your previous season into the next one. Re-invent yourself along the way as you incorporate your new mindset. Be creative in your new phase of development so that you can squeeze every ounce of personal growth and learning out of each phase.

Turn-time

I was born in good ole' Louisville, Kentucky. When Kentucky Derby time rolls around, truth be told, I am more interested in gawking at the big hats, but I discovered something so profound about a horse race. A horse race is divided into three fractions. The first and third fractions are not the best indicators as to the horse's ability to win the race. The determining factor is in the second fraction, the transition toward the head for home, or what is better known as the "turn-time."[6] Races are won or lost in the "turn-time." The reason that turn-time is so important is that it is difficult for a horse to maintain its velocity and path while negotiating a turn. Many times horses give up at the point of turn-time. Anxiety sets in when they hear the stomping hooves coming up behind them or they have a hard time transitioning from leading with their right or left feet. Horses are not natural born leaders, so if they are not properly trained, they may shrink back to their natural instincts and second guess their ability to step out in front as the forerunner. But, if handled just right, turn-time can set a horse up for the big win.

I am convinced that the key to crossing the finish line of your next level is won or lost in your turn-time. The key lies within your ability to negotiate your transition with precision; shut out the noise of what is behind you and be fearless in your ability to take the lead in your own life. Your next level will not be determined by how you started or even how you ended – it is in the way that you transition turn-time – your head for home.

It is important to remember that by the time the horse is heading for home and turning the corner at turn-time, the horse has already been around that same curve many times. But this go-around is different. The same curve he has rounded before, this time is the last time he will make the turn because this time he is headed for home. You may have been around this corner before. You may feel like you have been stuck in the same old cycle, but I want to declare to you that this time is different. This is your turn-time – your head for home. If you feel like you have been trapped in the first fraction for way too long, you can turn this corner again and head for the finish line!

The way you transition makes all of the difference. It is easy to look at something that is ending and not recognize that is the beginning of something new. Your ability to get to the new beginning is dependent on your –turn-time – the middle ground – the head for home – not getting stuck in the transitional periods of your life. Transition is an evolution that can keep you stuck in the same place if it is not combined with upward movement.

Turn-time is impacted by stamina, focus and sometimes bold, counter-intuitive actions. The skills needed to move through turn-time successfully are honed by repetitive training. This preparation time is essential. I believe that everything you have been through up unto this point has been the groundwork that you need to set you up for success as you enter this turn-time, hit your stride and head for home for the big win of achieving your next level.

Lessons from Lamaze

When it comes to transitioning, I am reminded of three key Lamaze practices to birth a baby in the natural, which give clues as to how you can handle the transition. The first Lamaze healthy birth practice is to let labor begin on its own. When a woman's body is transitioning during labor, the more she relaxes and lets go, the easier the birthing process will be. Contractions are just her body's way of moving, shifting and expanding to give the baby a passageway from inside of her to outside of her. When we are birthing the next level of our purpose and destiny, the more we let go and surrender to the process, the easier it will be. Transition is often a more of a subtle adjustment than a leap.

The second Lamaze healthy birth practice is to walk, move around and change positions throughout labor. The word transition means a modification; a shift. To transition from one season to the next, from one phase of your destiny to the next, it involves a shift. Maybe there is a shift in your thinking or even a shift in locations that needs to take place. The shift puts a demand on your physical endurance, your mental capability, your emotional tenacity, and your spiritual stamina. The shift expands your limitations, but the shift makes room for more.

The third Lamaze healthy birth practice is to bring a loved one or a friend for continuous support. Friendships provide protection, provision, and partnership. The connection is key! The people we are connected to are key influencers in our life because they are the ones who will provide a support system for us as we transition. Be on the lookout for key connections during times of transition and be willing to make bold moves, even when they are out of your comfort zone.[7]

> *Philippians 1:6 says, "There has never been the slightest doubt in my mind that the God who started this great work in you would keep at it and bring it to a **flourishing finish** on the very day Christ Jesus appears." MSG [emphasis added]*

Eventually, my daughter did give birth to my sweet little granddaughter. She is more than I could have ever asked for. She is so amazing that I do not have the words to describe how much joy she brings to us all. If you are in transition... Move! Shift! Connect!

It will happen in its time; you will make it through transition and you will give birth to the next phase of development! God started it and He will keep at it and bring it to a **flourishing finish**!

Practice the art of transitioning with grace and ease. It will make the journey more enjoyable.

Angela Aja

Phase One

The Ordinary

Angela Aja

Chapter 4

The Ordinary

"There's no such thing as an ordinary life." Mark Twain

The first phase of development that every woman has an opportunity to walk in and pass through is *The Ordinary*. Moving along in the familiar, you are born into a life that is chosen for you. You settle into a life that requires little risk. You develop a repetitive day to day routine. You learn to silence your voice and lead a predictable life.

The Ordinary is marked by self-discovery, learning and growing. New beginnings abound in *The Ordinary* phase of development, but only to a certain extent. New beginnings lead to a humdrum life. Boredom sets in and you no longer have the sense of importance and satisfaction that you once felt. You begin to question your worth and value. This is the point where you begin to look outside of yourself for validation, significance, and fulfillment. Phrases like, "don't rock the boat" and "better safe than sorry" inform your decisions that comfortable is better than uncomfortable. You cultivate a safe and secure lifestyle. You create cycles of busyness to distract you from the aching desire for a life of extraordinary. Then guilt raises its ugly head. How could you secretly desire more when life is good? Who do you think you are to dream of an extraordinary life when your ordinary life is good enough?

The surface problem is that you begin to feel bored with life in the phase of *The Ordinary*. You feel like there has got to be more to life than just surviving, going through the motions, stuck and spinning your wheels. You become the woman you are supposed to be rather than whom you were created to be. You tirelessly work to fit into the mold that has been passed down to you from generations. You bury your deepest desires and longings, convincing yourself that they do not matter. Your lips utter the dreaded "F" word... "I'm FINE." You look in the mirror but see a faded reflection; emptiness staring back at you.

You become driven by the demands of others. You mutate into a people-pleaser, a perfectionist or a control-freak as an effort to maintain some sense of control. Keeping the hamster wheel turning becomes the daily objective. Life has been diminished to a circus act, just trying to keep all of the plates spinning in the air without crashing down. You eventually morph into a false version of whom you were created to be. You hide behind layers and layers of masks that you have tirelessly forged as an attempt to shroud the fact that you have no idea who lives under the stratums of disguises. You feel exhausted and depleted. You feel like a victim, powerless over your own life. Overwhelmed and underwhelmed rule and reign.

The secret problem is that as a woman, you often assume that your worth comes from what you do. However, true significance comes from who you are at your core, not what you do. Your true significance will only reveal itself in your ability to *be*. But, because you are a nurturer by nature, you give and give and give, yet neglect yourself. You assume that you need to put everyone else's needs before your own and to consider your wants, needs, and desires, is selfish. You presume that if you give to yourself then you are detracting from your quality of benevolence to others. Actually, quite the opposite is true. What does the stewardess say when you get on the airplane? What she says seems counterintuitive but her instructions are to put the mask on yourself first, even if you are sitting next to a small child.

Symptoms of a woman in *The Ordinary* phase of development can span a wide range, from restlessness to resentment. You tend toward over-apologizing, over-giving and then feel overlooked. Life unfolds with dull beginnings. Dull turns into disregarded. Disregarded leads to desperation. A frantic need for approval and validation leads to negative self-talk. Feeling undervalued and underappreciated paves the way for unmet expectations. Inadequacy leads to indifference which becomes a front-runner to a full-on identity crisis. Stress, anxiety, and relationships that are suffering are par for the course. Finally, numbness detaches you from the reality of your current situation and coping becomes sufficient for keeping your head above water.

One day you wake up and an ordinary life has cemented you in place. Soon your life becomes unrecognizable.

Overlooked and Under-qualified

In *The Ordinary* phase of development, you feel overlooked and under-qualified. One of my favorite Bible stories reveals that being disregarded and discounted can be a set-up for success. In 1 Samuel, you find a story about how God raised up David to rule over His people. God instructed Samuel to call on a man named Jesse who had many sons, strapping young men who would fit all of the qualifications for the making of a king. He asked Jesse to line up all of his sons so that God could tell Samuel which one would become the king.

Here is how the story goes: starting in verse 6,

> "When they arrived, Samuel took one look at Jesse's son, Eliab and thought, 'Here he is! God's anointed!' 7 But God told Samuel, "Looks aren't everything. Don't be impressed with his looks and stature. I've already eliminated him. God judges a person differently than humans do. Men and women look at the face; God looks into the heart." MSG

Verse eight goes on to tell us that Jesse presented several of his sons to Samuel but Samuel knew that even though they had all of the right qualifications, they were not the one that God had chosen to be king. There was still one son that Samuel had not seen and who was not even in the line-up. David was in the back forty with the sheep – completely overlooked and under-qualified.

In verse 12, Samuel took one look at David and God said,

> "Up on your feet! Anoint him! This is the one." 13 Samuel took his flask of oil and anointed him, with his brothers standing around watching. The Spirit of God entered David like a rush of wind, God vitally empowering him for the rest of his life. MSG

It is easy to forget that God does not call the equipped, He equips the called. You might feel insignificant and under-qualified to fulfill your purpose. David was not the tallest, most handsome or the one with the biggest muscles. He was completely disregarded; he wasn't even invited to the line-up of sons. But God saw through the row of physically qualified young men, over the hills, past the forest, to a small field where one under-qualified boy sat with the sheep. That is whom He chose to be the king!

No matter what your stature, no matter what your level of physical, mental or emotional qualifications, you have a purpose that is bigger than you so that you will not rely solely on your own efforts. You have a mighty purpose. Instead of discounting yourself for the qualifications that you do not have, focus on what you do have. If you have felt overlooked and under-qualified, congratulations! You are perfect for the job! You may feel like a caterpillar but you house the DNA of a soaring butterfly.

My Life in *"The Ordinary"*

I made a nice comfy home in the midst of *The Ordinary*, too comfy of a home, as a matter of fact. I had felt overlooked and under-qualified, living in the shadows of a man. I spent 40 years in *The Ordinary*, much like how the children of Israel wandered in the desert for 40 long years. Culinary school got this little caterpillar moving along her path. It stirred a giant inside of me. For the first time in years, I began to consider me. I started thinking about what I wanted out of life. It was a great time of awakening for me. It aroused my God-given passion and abilities that had been lying dormant for so long.

When passion is ignited it impacts all areas of your life. Cooking was a passion that unleashed a potential that I had not even realized. It had been buried underneath years of self-neglect and lack of self-belief. I finished cooking school and started my own catering business.

One weekend, I packed up the car as I prepared to cater an out-of-town event. I remember the moment well. I hugged and kissed the kids because I would be gone overnight. My husband of twenty-two years was sitting on the couch in the family room. I walked in to give him a kiss and say goodbye. As I bent down to kiss him, he turned his head and offered me his cheek. So, I kissed his cheek. When I said, "I love you!" he replied, "Be safe." This was highly unusual because we said "I love you" to each other at least twenty times a day. I do not think it hit me until I was driving in the car, but all of a sudden, a feeling of despair washed over me. I recounted what had just taken place. That was not our normal exchange. That was not the way we operated. I was sick in the pit of my stomach. It was so hard to concentrate as I was preparing all of the food for this big event.

Things had been awry for several years previous. Lots of drama had ensued. Unfaithfulness had entered our marriage. I walked in forgiveness, stood in faith for my marriage and tried to use everything I had been through to grow as a person. I was committed to my wedding vows and I was determined to walk in the footsteps of my grandparents who were married for over 68 years. Divorce was not even an option that I had considered available to me. I believed with all of my heart that God would see us through and the previous few years would become a distant memory. But something was different this time.

While driving home after the weekend was over, I could hardly stay on the road due to the fountain of tears that came pouring out of me. Somehow, I knew my life was about to change forever. I was dreading the conversations that would face me when I got home. I wanted desperately to keep on driving into the sunset and escape the reality of what felt like impending doom. As I was driving and praying, seeking Divine guidance, I felt the hands of God on my shoulders. I could sense God's presence and I was suddenly reminded that He had my back. As crazy as it sounds, I felt God lift a burden off my shoulders. Suddenly, a peace came over me and inner confidence rose up on the inside and I knew that I could handle whatever was to come.

The most difficult conversations of my life took place when I returned home that day. What I had feared the most had come upon me. My marriage of twenty-two years was ending. He had fallen in love with another woman.

My older two children were old enough to be on their own. We had been through financial devastation; bankruptcy, the repossession of our home and cars, the loss of our churches and so much more. We had sold most of our furniture just to make ends meet, so there was nothing to fight over, nothing to divide. After twenty-two years of marriage, I packed up my belongings and moved into an apartment with my two youngest sons. We moved in with a TV, a computer, an end table, and a queen size mattress. For the next three months, the boys and I ate on the floor, slept on the floor and played Yahtzee on the floor. I had no idea how I was going to support us. All I knew was that our lives would never be the same.

My entire identity had been built on a foundation of supporting a man in the pursuit of his dreams and being in the ministry. My parents were pastors all throughout my childhood. I was raised in the church, went to bible college, married a pastor and then became a pastor; an ordained minister. Because of my divorce, with the exception of my parents and my sister, the support system that I had grown accustomed to, the church, no longer supported me. I was marked with the stigma of divorce. I went from preaching in the pulpit to warming the pews, which turned into sitting in my pajamas. My ordinary life had come to an end.

Transformation always involves transition. A transition is a realignment; a shift. Movement is a part of transition. I felt alone, I felt abandoned and I felt hopeless. However, there was a spark of the essence of transformation down deep on the inside of me.

Stuck in *The Ordinary*

A woman is meant to pass through *The Ordinary*, she is not meant to stay there. Too often though, change can feel frightening and succumbing to *staying put* can result in getting stuck in a season instead of moving through it. What does life look like if you have gotten stuck in *The Ordinary*? Being trapped in the first phase of development can occur when you do not allow the setback to beckon you into *The Cave*. Even though there is no allure to *The Cave*, it is a vital step in a woman's journey toward *The Rise*. *The Cave* and the grave can feel squeamishly similar but what happens in *The Cave* produces an undeniable transformation.

Fear of the unknown, fear of risk and fear of letting go of the woman you have become can keep you stuck in a life of ordinary. Low-quality questions consume your thoughts. What if you let go of the woman you have become and the woman that you are meant to be is no better? What if the woman you are meant to become is not really there? What if she is a figment of your imagination? What if the woman who lives outside of the ordinary has fears, failures, and disappointments? Letting go of your ordinary life involves risk and getting comfortable with being uncomfortable.

Therein lies the problem…extraordinary is in each and every woman, haunting her and taunting her with a picture of the seeds of greatness that are inside of her. Every woman, if she looks in the mirror deep enough can see glimpses of her royal crown. When you mask your purpose with busyness, fear and a "dumbed down" version of yourself, you get as many plates spinning up in the air as possible and create drama just so you can feel alive.

A woman who has not developed past *The Ordinary* often times feels as though she has settled. I remember crying myself to sleep at night knowing that I was merely surviving. I remember being stuck in *The Ordinary* phase. I felt like I was in the movie

"Groundhog's Day" where the same scenario played over and over again. I kept re-creating the same problems and getting the same results. Finally, one day I looked at my mom as I was crying and I remember saying to her, "I feel like I don't fit into my own life." It seemed so menial but yet so excruciating at the same time. That is when I realized that it was time for me graduate and succumb to the unavoidable – *The Cave*. *The Cave* is the second phase of development that every woman has the opportunity to pass through.

Life in *The Ordinary* resembles the life of a caterpillar destined to become a butterfly. In the following chapter, you will read about the correlation and gain insight into your own journey of transformation.

Let me add a small disclaimer here. It does not have to take divorce and devastation to move you into *The Cave.* Any setback that awakens you to the possibility of whom you were created to be can compel you into the dark, lonely phase of purposeful preparation known as *The Cave.*

Chapter 5

The Caterpillar

"I want to be like a caterpillar. Eat a lot, sleep for a while and then wake up beautiful." Author Unknown

*L*ife begins in *The Ordinary*. Moving along in the familiar, you are born into a life that is chosen for you. Your personality develops and experiences begin to shape you as you inch through life as a hungry little caterpillar, taking in as much of life as you can. You feed on the experiences of joy and sorrow, pleasure and pain. Your tendency to avoid pain begins at an early age. You become adept in the art of self-protection and self-preservation.

The Ordinary is a season that mimics the expedition of the inchworm, better known as a caterpillar on its journey to escalation. The caterpillar season is marked by limited vision and restricted mobility. A caterpillar has beady little eyes that can only see what is directly in front of her. During this phase of life, you may find yourself consumed by the tyranny of the urgent. You may find yourself feeling limited and constrained by the daily grind, wondering if this is all there is to life.

Life may feel like it is dragging on as if you are stuck in the mundane, menial tasks of everyday life just like a fuzzy caterpillar who has limited mobility due to her tiny, little legs. This season may be marked by low-level thinking and a nagging internal conversation that "there has got to be more to life than this." You have inklings that there is more, but you feel guilty because life is basically good. Something inside of you longs for a life of *extraordinary* yet you are trapped in an ordinary life.

Caterpillars spend most of their time hiding in trees, blending in with their environment.[8] You know that you are in *The Ordinary* when you realize that you have camouflaged your true nature as a way of self-protection. It may have become easier to stay in hiding rather than speak your truth. You may show signs of having morphed into whom you are *supposed* to be rather than who you really are. This season is usually marked by insecurity and insignificance, measuring your self-worth by what you see on the surface. Even though life feels hard, it is all you know, so you carry on as usual.

The interesting thing about a caterpillar is that the DNA of a butterfly is wrapped up inside of the caterpillar. As a caterpillar eats and moseys through life, she is not trying to become something different; she is compelled to transform into who she really is. The body of a caterpillar is just the container for the most authentic version of whom she was originally created to be. There is a holy dissatisfaction that begins to churn down on the inside of a woman in *The Ordinary* phase of life, awakening the DNA of a queen – a butterfly on the rise. There is an instinctive process that begins to compel her toward seclusion so that she can become the highest version of herself.

My Life as a Caterpillar

It was mid-2012 and my daughter was away in college at Texas Tech University. She had been able to escape the reality of our changing family dynamics, even if it was for a semester at a time.

She and I, however, kept our normal routine of talking at least once a day intact. I remember having a conversation with her one day that would change me forever. I knew that she could hear the stress in my voice. I knew it scared her, but we had a ritual. When she was down, I would encourage her and remind her that God was faithful and that He would see us through all of this. On the flip side, when I was discouraged and overwhelmed, she would remind me of the same. There was usually plenty of laughter, tears and "I love you's," and then we would hang up the phone refreshed and ready to take on whatever was next. But this time was different. I had felt a slow expiring taking place inside of me. I was getting tired and weary. There was a numbness that was overtaking my being and I did not know how to wake myself up. I was in survival mode, but just surviving felt immobilizing. It was beginning to feel like death and I knew she was beginning to sense it.

After my marriage had ended, it left me feeling small and insignificant, wanting to hide from my past. However, something kept compelling me. I became like a little caterpillar in the larva stage. During the larva stage or the feeding stage, the main job of the caterpillar is to eat and grow. The caterpillar can grow up to 100 times its size and shed its skin four to five times during this stage. This is where the nourishment comes from for the upcoming transition stage as it enters into the cocoon. I found myself, like a hungry caterpillar, ready to try new things and experience the world in a whole new way. I got out and made new friends and new connections with people. I was ready to taste what the world had to offer.

Suddenly, I found myself as the sole provider for myself and my kids. Up until that point, I had really only worked in the ministry. But, just like a hungry caterpillar, I had an appetite to get out and try new ways to provide for my family. So, I worked in the door-to-door window sales business, the roofing business, and the wine-tasting business. I worked at William Sonoma, setting up displays in the middle of the night. I did catering and personal chef work. For a short time, I was a caregiver to the elderly and the disabled and an insurance salesman. I even worked as a bouncer for one weekend (funny, but true.) Later on, I got a good, stable job in the oil and gas industry. I felt myself growing as a person, and like the growing caterpillar, shedding its skin; I was shedding layers of fear, self-doubt, and insecurities. I was taking on new challenges and creating a new identity.

In the midst of it all, I remembered a story about what an old Indian tribe would do as they went into battle. This particular tribe of warriors would run out onto the battlefield with their weapon in one hand and a stake with a rope tied to one end in the other hand. Once they got to the middle of the battlefield, they would tie the rope around their ankle and drive the stake into the ground. Their approach was that they would either live there or die there. That was my mindset. Life felt more like a battlefield during those times, trying to provide for my kids and help them heal. My hardest battle was always my finances. I had to defend my family against hunger and poverty and I would either live there or die there on that battlefield. Somehow, I knew that if I drove the stake in the ground, everything I had been through up unto that point would give me the fortitude to live there and be victorious.

In the midst of what felt like a battle, I laid my past down for a little while and jumped into my new identity as a single woman with both feet, as if I was jumping into a crystal-clear pond on a hot summer day. I met some single moms in the apartment complex where I lived who showed me the ropes at riding solo. Sharing the same name, we referred to them as "The Karen's". They were beautiful, vibrant and highly skilled at the single life. We became a support system for each other, helping each other out with our kids, who were all the same age and in the same grade. We shared much laughter and many tears. After living most of my life as a married woman, "The Karen's," taught me that being single can be fun and full. Had I not met them, I think I would have thought that being single meant living a lonely and drab life. They showed me how to move through this new life with autonomy and self-sufficiency.

I was enjoying taking a swim in this new pond of single living. Being married for 22 years, I had never once wanted to be single, but since this was my new swimming hole, I decided to learn how to swim here rather than drown. I learned how to be a fighter. I learned how to survive. This was a double-edged sword, however, jumping right in and acting as if my life had not just been through a monsoon. On one hand, I was happy and enjoying all of the experience's life was handing me. On the other hand, there was an empty cavern in my soul that I had been ignoring that felt more like the black hole than a refreshing swimming hole. There was still a darkness that I avoided daily.

The art of surviving is a wonderful gift from God, but at some point, if surviving does not turn into thriving, stagnation occurs. The once clear pond of crisp, cool water turns to muck and mire, producing a swampy feel. This is what my life was beginning to feel like. I was numb. I had not healed. I was getting weary on the battlefield. I was going through the motions, trying to keep my head above water. Now, where I had once played freely, there was moss and unwanted creatures sharing my pond.

It was at this point in my life, that the memorable conversation with my daughter occurred. Even when you have become highly skilled at the art of surviving, you cannot fool the ones who love you the most; the ones you are connected with soul to soul. My kids are my soulmates and your soulmates cannot be fooled. Ashley knew me for the clear, refreshing water that I had been and she even had the audacity to remind me that the swamp that I had become was not who I truly was. I will always be grateful to her for that. She spoke words that went straight through my soul, like a knife; cutting me, but healing me at the same time. On the other end of the phone she said tearfully, "Mommy, where are you? It is like you are there but you are not there. I want you back." I remember feeling such desperation because I wanted to come back to life. I wanted the numbness to go away. I wanted to shake myself like you shake your foot when it falls asleep. But I resisted it too, I knew that if I would shake myself to wake myself, there would be pins and needles, just like shaking a numb foot.

I realized at that moment I had stayed in my stupor long enough. I could sense change was coming and I was ready for it. I was ready for the pins and needles; I was ready to wake up and I was ready to feel again, even if it meant feeling the pain I had been avoiding. I was ready to climb out of the swamp of unforgiveness, rejection, and pain and go into my cocoon and let nature take its course. Just like the hungry little caterpillar who inherently knows that the increased appetite and shedding of the old skin is due to the change that is coming, I became aware that where I was, at that moment in time, was not my final dwelling place. I was not born to inch my way through life like a caterpillar, merely surviving. I was not placed on this earth just to eat and grow. Somewhere in my DNA, the ability to fly and soar to new heights wanted to be unleashed. Somewhere in the depths of me, my butterfly was calling me into a season of healing; a place where I could be transformed and fitted with wings. I was ready to surrender to the only place where that could take place... inside of the cocoon.

As 2012 came to end, I truly wanted to leave behind those things which would no longer benefit me and move forward. I wanted to start the process of going from surviving to thriving. Even though 2012 was a good year overall, one of the nagging feelings that were prevalent was disappointment. I saw the evidence of disappointment show up in my relationships, my business, and my purpose. Things that I thought were going to happen never happened. Doors that looked like they had opened up seemed to slam shut at the last minute. People that said they were going to come through never did.

In order to understand disappointment, first, we must look at the root word, which is "appointment."[9] It means "the choice of somebody for the job or a position."[10] Disappointment is a feeling that there has been a reversal from the position I was appointed to. The only way that I knew how to leave disappointment behind was to remember the position to which I had been appointed from the beginning.

While disappointment can be caused by many things, I knew that the root of my feelings of disappointment had been directly linked to my divorce. I grew up in a family where parents and grandparents stayed married until "death do us part." I also grew up with the notion that I would live happily ever after with the one I had married. I was left with this desperate feeling that somehow because of the divorce, the former plan and purpose that I had been called to had been reversed and that all of my efforts had been wasted. I felt like I had disappointed my children, my parents, myself, the church and God. Honestly, I also felt disappointed by God.

January of 2013 had marked three years of being divorced. When I think about the number three, I think about closure. When you have three lines, it is the first time you can put them together to create something that is enclosed...a triangle. I somehow knew that 2013 not only represented closing the door to the past but also the opening of new doors. In those last three years, I had seen God's love, grace and mercy prevail in my life and I was so grateful for the journey that I had been able to walk through. I had met so many incredible people and had so many fun experiences along the way that had made my life so rich and robust. I had grown and expanded but that nagging feeling of disappointment haunted me and kept me from walking into the fullness that I knew I was destined for. I was finally ready to fully close the door to the past and remember the things I had been appointed for.

The word "divorce" means to separate or distinguish something from something else. As I left behind 2012 and moved into 2013, I was going to give "divorce" a new meaning in my life. I was divorcing myself from disappointment. Disappointment had been like a deadbeat, mentally abusive lover that would not go away. I kicked him out and left all of his belongings out on the street. Disappointment and I could no longer cohabitate! After all of the DISAPPOINTMENT, I knew I had an APPOINTMENT to keep!

My Divine Appointment with the Prophetess at the Resale Shop

In January of 2013, after work one day, right after my conversation with my daughter, I had the urge to buy a desk so that I could get a little more organized. I wanted somewhere to sit and do my work, other than the dining room table. I set out on a mission. My first stop was the local Goodwill, which "The Karen's" and I sneakily called "GW." I had a gut feeling that I would find my desk at a nominal price at GW. I walked to the back of the store where they kept their furniture but no desks in sight. One of the ladies who worked there saw the discouragement on my face and asked me what I was looking for. I told her and she said, "Oh, you need to go across the street to that little resale shop over there." I had seen that one but I had never been in there. I got in my car and off I went, continuing on with my mission.

I pulled into the parking lot across the street from GW, got out of my car and ran for the door as fast as I could. Just as I walked through the door, a lady darted behind me, grabbed the door and locked it. She said, "Whew, you made it in here just in time. We are getting ready to close for the night." I smiled, grateful that I had made it over the threshold. As I stepped further into the store to take a closer look around, there it was; my desk, exactly as I had imagined it. It was in the back of the store, drawing me in, as if it had a beacon of light, calling me toward it.

As I made a direct line for the desk, all of a sudden, from behind the dress rack, stepped a beautiful black woman, dressed to the nines. Her stature was tall and regal. There was an air of confidence about her and I immediately knew she was on a mission from God. Our eyes met and our souls connected as if we had known each other for years. She stepped right into my path and stuck out her hand to shake mine. She studied me for a few seconds and then told me I was beautiful. Somehow when she told me I was beautiful, I knew she saw the inside of me, not just my outer appearance. I knew she could see something in my eyes. She saw through the darkness and straight to the spark of light that was buried under all of the pain and devastation.

As if seeing this beautiful black woman standing in front of me was not intriguing enough, what she said next sealed the deal for me. She said with a sense of authority, "We need to talk! God wants you to know it's not over! Everything you have been through is about to be turned around." My mouth was hanging open so wide; I swear I could feel my bottom lip touch the ground. We quickly exchanged numbers as store employees were encouraging us to finish making our purchases. I walked out of the store that day with tears in my eyes and a smile that went from ear to ear. I knew God had parted the heavens that day to give me a message and to let me know that He still had a plan for me. Even though my life had not turned out as I expected, I saw a glimpse of purpose from my pain. While I was in my caterpillar phase, she saw my wings and spoke directly to my butterfly.

Jeremiah 29:11 says, "For I know the plans I have for you," declares the Lord, a plan to prosper you and not to harm you, plans to give you a hope and a future." NIV

I walked out of that resale shop with my desk, but greater than that, I walked out with a renewed sense of hope. I did not know if I would ever hear from her again, but it did not matter. She had been the mouthpiece of God for me that day.

That night my phone rang at 2:00 a.m. Having grown children, it has been my experience that when your phone rings at 2:00 a.m., it is probably one of them and your presence is required in some way. I sat straight up in bed, waiting to hear what drama was about to ensue. To my surprise, I heard a familiar voice on the other end. It was the prophetess from the resale shop. Yes, she called me in the middle of the night, and every night thereafter for the next three weeks, praying for me and speaking life over me. She would call me "Woman of God." (No one had called me "Woman of God" for a very long time.) Several times, she even told me that she had her whole prayer team back in Georgia, up in the middle of the night praying for me. I am convinced that if God had not sent her to pray for me and encourage me, I would not have made it through the next season of my life, the cocoon stage, the way that I did. Several months later, she would ask me to come and speak to her congregation. I accepted the offer and spoke about my life as a butterfly, which became the birthplace of this book.

This had been my season of gathering and feeding, just like the caterpillar in the larva stage. Something inside of me knew that all of my eating and growing would be the nourishment I would need for what was coming next. My environment began to change and that could only mean one thing…I was headed into the cocoon.

Chapter 6

The Crisis

"When written in Chinese, the word "crisis" is composed of two characters. One represents danger and the other represents opportunity." John F. Kennedy

Smack dab in the middle of *The Ordinary*, that is when a setback occurs. A setback can show up in the form of a crisis, a tragedy or any obstacle that impedes you from moving forward. A setback is an external event that steps into the middle of *The Ordinary* and stirs the pot. A predicament comes along and causes a commotion bringing awareness that *The Ordinary* is not your final resting place. A setback has a way of driving you into the cocoon of seclusion. Whether its abandonment, rejection, betrayal, death, divorce or loss – the death of who you were is imminent in order for you to be reborn into whom you are at your core.

The reason that a setback rocks you at your core is because you have given peripheral events the power to prove who you are or who you are not. You derive meaning about your significance from your external surroundings. If you are broke then you are worthless. If you fail then you are a failure. If someone walks out of your life then you are not worth loving. The dark night of our soul comes in the form of a setback to drive you into a space where we can re-evaluate your identity, reclaim your values and restate your purpose.

Queen Esther

Esther was an ordinary girl growing up in ordinary surroundings. Her given name was Hadassah. Hadassah means myrtle and the myrtle tree was a symbol of God's promise. The crisis of losing her mother and father laid the foundation for her to be taken out of the familiar and into a court of women, in the king's palace where a metamorphosis would take place. Hadassah may not have been qualified to be the queen, but the process of development that she endured ultimately prepared her for the position that she was destined for as Queen Esther. Hadassah's loss positioned her to be relocated to her place of purpose.

The Kingdom Works Backwards

Just as Hadassah's loss positioned her to be relocated to her place of purpose, your loss has prepared you for promotion. Setbacks occur to propel you forward. To move out of an ordinary life into an extraordinary existence requires a new level of thinking. Being Kingdom minded works from the principle of an opposite flow. This type of "intentional opposite" rewires of the brain, stripping the former meaning of words and phrases down to the core so that new meaning can be attached.

It is easy to get into a habit of labeling things as good/bad, right/wrong and either/or. But what about both/and? To think in terms of good/bad, right/wrong and either/or is to think from an earthly perspective. It leaves no room for grace. To think in terms of both/and, new doors of opportunity reveal themselves immediately. You can see things you have been overlooking the whole time.

Let's look at a few examples of a Kingdom mindset working in reverse:

- *Matthew 5:44a says, "But I say to you, love your enemies, bless those who curse you, do good to those who hate you, and pray for those who spitefully use you and persecute you." NKJV*

The mindset shift is to forgo revenge and operate at a whole new level.

- *Matthew 5:39 says, "But I tell you not to resist an evil person. But whoever slaps you on your right cheek, turn the other to him also" NKJV*

Normally, if someone slaps you it presents an opportunity for physical and emotional pain. The strike is a display of intense contempt, but to turn the other cheek is to remove the contemptible meaning from the strike thereby taking away its power. So, in essence, the strike loses its negative connotation and "to turn the other cheek" becomes an act of service.

- *Luke 6:38 says, "Give, and it will be given to you: good measure, pressed down, shaken together, and running over will be put into your bosom. For with the same measure that you use, it will be measured back to you." NKJV*

Give and it will be given unto you – The old mindset is that if you give, you are losing something, but the new mindset is to give and when you give, you will get more. The shift is in the mindset and causes a different physical outcome. It is possible to give more and add more value without being diminished in any way.

- *Matthew 5:40 says," If anyone wants to sue you and take away your tunic, let him have your cloak also." NKJV*

To go above and beyond what is being asked of you is the Kingdom mindset that strips the power of lack and deficiency.

- *1 Peter 3:9 says, "not returning evil for evil or reviling for reviling, but on the contrary blessing, knowing that you were called to this, that you may inherit a blessing." NKJV*

A natural reaction to a malicious act is to do the same in return but the Kingdom mindset is to repay an insult with a blessing.

- *Matthew 20:16 says, "So the last will be first, and the first last." NKJV*

In most circumstances, to be first is deemed a noble feat. There is a grandiose feeling of achievement that accompanies being the originator. To be last denotes failure or lacking the ability to measure up, at the very least. However, to consider that the act of being last is more desirable causes a riveting jolt to your old way of thinking about positioning. A Kingdom mindset promises that position is not an indicator of advantage.

These are mind-blowing concepts. The big takeaway here is that a setback offers you a place of solitude so that you can reconsider the meaning that you have given to life. What you may have deemed as harmful becomes helpful in your development.

Take your life story, for example. What if there was some *good* wrapped up within the parts of your story that you have been labeling as *bad*? What if there was a certain amount of *right* tangled in with what you have labeled as *wrong*? What if you began to see the *bad* parts of your story as *good* and the *right* and *wrong* were intertwined into a poetic tale of love and loss, beauty and horror. If you come from the perspective of either/or instead of both/and, then you miss out on the beauty that can come from your ashes.

Let me explain further with a story about a client of mine. I have changed her name and gotten permission to share her story. Bridget was going through my twelve-week program. When we first began, she was riddled with guilt and shame about decisions she had made as a young woman. She viewed her decisions as reckless and made a promise to herself that playing it safe was the way she would protect herself from heartache and pain. But this was causing a problem for her because her *reckless* nature was actually one of her greatest gifts that God had given her. Because of her hasty decisions as a young woman, she labeled herself as reckless and she labeled reckless as bad. She was beginning to feel bored and irritable with life because she was not being authentic.

In one of our sessions, as I heard the cry of her heart from underneath all of the masks that she had layered on as an attempt to stay *safe* from her reckless self, I ask her a question that cut like a surgical knife and revealed the most precious gift of who God had created her to be. I asked her, "Bridget, when did you decide that *safe* was the more desirable way to live?" The silence was thick and then came the tears; a week of healing tears, to be exact. Bridget had a life-changing aha-moment that day and recounted all of the ways that she had kept herself stuck in The *Ordinary* by labeling a part of who she had been created to be as *bad*.

Bridget embraced her reckless nature, realizing that it was a gift from God and a key component of the giftings and abilities that she was born with to be able to fulfill her life purpose. She renamed *reckless* as bold, brave, adventurous and daring. Bridget is now showing up in the world as her authentic self and making things happen that she never dreamed she would be able to do. Bridget is a world-changing, risk-taking woman who is letting her light shine through the gift of whom God created her to be and I am proud to call her my friend. She took what she had previously labeled as *wrong* or *bad* and turned it around to *right* and *good*.

Setbacks come in the form of crisis. Setbacks are usually accompanied by pain, whether mental, physical or emotional. Setbacks are often uncomfortable seasons of life that bring you face to face with a decision; a decision to become the victim of your circumstances or to take advantage of an opportunity that thrusts you into your next level as the victorious overcomer that you were created to be. A setback is nothing more than a setup for a comeback. Setbacks compel you into the cocoon – *The Cave* of development where transformation takes place.

Setbacks throw you into survival mode. I remember being a dorky, awkward teenager, dancing around my room with a hairbrush for a microphone in-hand, lip-syncing Gloria Gaynor's "I Will Survive,"[11] but my inner diva was being strengthened, all the while. I did not realize the impact that this disco song would have on my life. It would become an anthem that would carry me through some of the most turbulent times of my life. Gloria's message of moving on, no matter what you have been through, got deep down inside of me and resurfaced, later in my life, right when I needed it the most. After my crisis, somehow, I instinctively knew that I had to survive.

After my setback, things were not easy. There were many days I did not know how I was going feed my kids or keep a roof over our heads. And the pain...the pain felt like it was ripping a hole right through my heart. The embarrassment, the disappointment, the loneliness, and the disillusionment sometimes felt like never-ending closed-fisted blows from a boxer defending his title. It felt like my dreams had been shattered and my purpose had been ripped out of my hands. It was as if I was in a fight for my life, a fight for my sanity and a fight for my destiny. But, being a survivor, it brought out strength and a tenacity that I never realized I had. Although my invisible opponent taunted me with resentment and anger, he underestimated my will, resilience, and endurance. I knew if I could just stay in the ring and not throw in the towel, I could outlast this unseen adversary that was trying to keep me pinned up against the ropes of my past.

Why do we feel such a strong urge to survive? Why do we fight as if we were in the ring, enduring even the most powerful punches of betrayal and disappointment?

The word "survive," according to the Encarta Dictionary, means *to not die or disappear.*[12] It means *to live through something.* We were born to live our lives in the spotlight of love and forgiveness, not hiding in the shadowy corner of disloyalty and dissatisfaction that make us want to disappear into the mundane. It is instinctive for us to get back up again when we have been knocked down, even when we think we hear the referee bellow out the final countdown.

What is good about the fight? What is so great about survival? Survival is a God-given impulse that thrusts us to what comes after surviving...and that is thriving. To thrive is to increase, to flourish and to walk in a new level of success. A caterpillar that can merely inch its way along the ground, has to survive the dark, tight confinement of the cocoon before it transforms into a butterfly with wings that gives it the ability to move at an accelerated speed than it previously did. A seed, surrounded by dirt and darkness is altered into a new form as new life struggles to burst forth from the outer shell that kept it impounded in a smaller state of being. Survival transforms us into something new. Survival brings out our creativity. Survival opens our minds to new possibilities and causes us to think outside of the box. Survival elevates our vision to new heights. Survival stirs up compassion. Survival unveils our purpose.

You cannot live in survival mode forever. At some point, you will need to shift gears and move into thriving but surviving has its place. While survival may serve you well during a crisis, you cannot stay there. Going through the full process of development demands a modification.

Unless you want to be stuck in *The Ordinary*, the only thing you can do is to surrender to the wooing of *The Cave*. While yielding may feel like utter defeat, it is not! It is a willing release of who you were so that you can become the fullest expression of who you are. Abandon yourself with full consent to the evolution that is beckoning you so that the proliferation of your purpose can be revealed. Grant yourself permission to the decomposition of *The Cave* so that the evolution of whom you were created to be can be fully established. To escape the confinement of *The Ordinary*, death to the normal, ordinary events of a monotonous existence is imminent.

It is time to acquiesce to *The Cave* of transformation.

Angela Aja

Phase Two

The Cave

Angela Aja

Chapter 7

The Cave

"The cave you fear to enter holds the treasure you seek." Joseph Campbell

Every year I ask God to give me a word, just one word for the year. I knew that 2013 would be a year of divine appointments but I knew that my word for the year was "LEAP." I had declared 2013 to be my leap year. I was not exactly sure what I was leaping to or leaping from, but I knew that it would become clear.

After growing up with pastors for parents, being married right out of bible college and being involved in the ministry all of my life, I did not know anything about life outside of the church. After my divorce, I found myself in a strange new place. For the first time, I had to think about what I wanted to do with the rest of this time I had here on earth. I had created an identity that included everyone else but me. I had to look in the mirror and ask myself questions like, "What do you want out of life?" "What do you want to experience?" "What dreams still need to become a reality?" and even "What do you like and dislike?"

Upon entering the single world, I decided to get a little hipper so I created a Facebook page. (Of course, this made my kids nervous!) Up until that point, I had created a safe life for myself. Afraid to speak up, afraid to disagree, making sure everyone else was happy and following their dreams. I was living out my motto for life that it was better to be safe than sorry. So, in this new phase of life, I chose my favorite quote as my mantra to live by. John A. Shedd said,

"A ship in harbor is safe, but that is not what ships are built for."

I guess I related to those words of wisdom, feeling like I had been anchored at a harbor, but now I was ready to be launched out into the deep. Hoist the sails! Bring on the winds and the waves!

Ha! What in the world was I thinking? Believe me, the old saying is true, "Be careful what you ask for!" Well, guess what... three years later, there I was recovering from seasickness, being water-logged and maybe even a little bit of scurvy (all figuratively, of course.) I lived that motto, getting out of my comfort zone and out into the deep waters of experience.

My Ship Was Coming into Harbor

After three years of my new single life, my ship was finally arriving at a new port. It is time for me to refuel, restock, allow some of the barnacles to be scraped off and even get a fresh coat of paint. Life had felt like turbulent seas but I was ready to drop my anchor at my new port of call in The Woodlands, Texas. In the spring of 2013, God had opened the door for me there for a full time, steady job where I would be able to bring some stability to my family. I leaped into a position in the oil and gas industry without hesitation and it was a smooth transition.

There was no doubt in my mind that God had me in Austin, Texas for a reason. While in Austin, I experienced some of the most turbulent times of my life, but also the most cherished! Yes, there had been pirates (people) along the way, but there had also been treasure (people) along the way. I am so thankful for the experiences and relationships that I had made in Austin. Those experiences and relationships prepared me for what was coming next, but my time had ended there. I had declared that 2013 would be a year of appointments. Moving to Houston proved to be a docking station filled with divine appointments but ultimately became the place of my new residence in *The Cave*. Somehow, I knew that I would be called on to put my "sea legs" on again someday, but I decided next time I hit the high seas; I'm goin' out on a cruise ship!

The Cave

A cave is a hollowed-out place in the ground that serves as a home for animals. It provides protection and respite for the hibernating kind. A cave usually has only one point of entrance and burrows deep into the belly of the earth. A cave is an excavated cavern. Caves provide food, solace, protection, hiding places as well as being a place to bury the dead.

There are three prominent stories about significant cave dwellers in the Bible that offer insight into the happenings of the phase of development that I call "The Cave." There are three lessons to be learned about our cave experience. First, "The Cave" phase in your life represents a hidden base of operations where personal transformation can take place. Second, there is a price to be paid for this full process of development and our commitment to remain a cave-dweller until our cave season is over is of utmost importance. Third, you'll know when you are being called out of the cave.

1 Samuel, Chapter 22, tells the story of The Cave of Adullam. David had been chosen out of the line-up of all of his brothers to become the next king of Israel. But Saul, the current king was very jealous of David and set out on a pursuit to kill David before he could become king. So, David was on the run. He came upon the Cave of Adullam. Adullam means a headquarters, a refuge or a retreat. This cave became his base of operations; it was his hidden conservatoire of kingly preparedness.[13]

The Cave is a hidden retreat for the purpose of preparation. When you are in *The Cave* phase of development, it is important to embrace your new base of operations – your headquarters of loneliness. This veiled season is your transformational training academy. It is an incubation period and a departure of the norm for the purpose of advancement. It is possible to be alone and not lonely in this season if you are fully aware of the promotion that you are being equipped for. Lay hold of this season of royal refuge and respite. You will find protection as you practice the art of your passion, potential, and purpose.

There is another cave in the Bible that sheds light on how to maneuver *The Cave* phase of development. Genesis, Chapter 23 tells a story of one of the patriarchs of old, Abraham. Sarah, Abraham's wife had died. Remember Sarah, who got pregnant when she was near 100 years old? Yes, that Sarah. Abraham had to bury his partner in life and in faith. He was in a foreign land and asked the owner of the land for the Cave of Machpelah to bury his wife. Ephron the Hittite, the owner of the land, offered to give the cave to Abraham at no charge. Abraham insisted on paying full price for the cave that would be a remembrance of his legacy.

When you are in *The Cave* phase of development, it is of the utmost importance to be willing to pay the full price for burying who you were so that you may become whom you were created to be. Letting go of the old comes at a cost. The price you pay for something is your commitment to it. Not everyone is willing to go through the full process of development but it is the commitment to the completion of transformation that will prepare you to soar to new heights.

The third story of a biblical cave is found in John, Chapter 11. Lazarus, a dear friend of Jesus, had died and been buried in a cave. He had been dead for four days. Mary and Martha, the sisters of Lazarus, had sent word to Jesus that his friend had died in hopes that their Lord would come and save the day. The Bible says that instead of running to their rescue, He stayed where He was for two more days and by the time Jesus had arrived, Lazarus had been dead for four days. Lazarus, being dead for four days, carries great significance in Jewish tradition. It was believed that the spirit of a dead man would linger for three days. By the fourth day, his spirit would have already left his body and there would be no hope for resurrection. The body would have also begun to decay, rendering the likelihood of rising from the dead not only impossible but undesirable. Who wants to be raised from the dead with a decaying body? However, in this story, Jesus waited until the situation was deemed utterly hopeless before He showed up and called Lazarus back to life and out of the grave.[14]

Many times, when you are in the middle of a cave experience you desperately want God to come and rescue you out of your pit but yet your time in *The Cave* lingers. At times it seems that God waits until things seem utterly and completely dead – absolutely no hope that the resurrection of our situation is even possible. Resurgence from *The Cave* does not happen at your command. *The Cave* experience is there to remind you that you will emerge from your season of transformation when the metamorphosis is complete – not when you decide you are done. There are no shortcuts in *The Cave*.

Commit to your transformational training academy. Be willing to pay the full price for the process of your development. Know that even if all hope seems lost, that is when you are perfectly positioned for a resurrection – a resurgence. *The Cave* phase of development is absolutely necessary for your comeback after a setback.

I remember my own cave experience well. There were many times that I cried and blamed God for abandoning me during my dark and lonely season of development. I touted how life was not fair and angrily asked God, "What did I do to deserve this?" I cannot tell you that I always handled myself above reproach in *The Cave*. But it was there that I learned to acquiesce. I had been in survival mode for so long that the dark night of my soul is where I learned to trust again – to trust God, trust others and to trust myself. My cave experience of development is where I honed the skills of emotional responsibility and emotional resilience.

There is no replacement for the process. A cave is a time of separation. A cave is a season of development. A cave is a season of acquiescing to the loss of whom you have become so that who you are at your core can rise to the surface. "The Cave" phase of development that every woman has an opportunity to walk through is similar to the metamorphosis that takes place in the cocoon. In the following chapter, you will read about the breakdown and reformation of the caterpillar into the butterfly that takes place in the cocoon. You will learn how it holds clues for us as we are renovated from the inside out in preparation for *The Rise*.

Chapter 8

The Cocoon

"God does His deepest work in our darkest hour." A.W. Tozer

The cave, the grave, and the cocoon are squeamishly similar. All three are dark, lonely vessels of isolation but the cocoon produces the necessary environment conducive for the purpose of preparation.

Once I got to The Woodlands, things changed dramatically. This once social butterfly morphed into a quiet, lonely existence. My surroundings were unfamiliar, yet safe. I was unacquainted with this type of loneliness. There were no friends to go out with; my older kids were far away. I went to work, made dinner, took care of Judson and lay on the couch watching TV. My favorite was, The Food Network, no less, enticing me to drown my sorrows in fat and sugar-laden delectable morsels that piled on the pounds. I did this day after day. I was making a steady income but I had less than I had ever had. Life felt trite and stale but for some reason, I knew I was exactly where I supposed to be. In this isolated place, it seemed as though my world had taken on an unfamiliar form. I had finally stopped running in avoidance of my cave experience. I said "YES!" and surrendered to my cave and spun the encasing of my cocoon where metamorphosis could begin.

When the caterpillar goes into the cocoon, it is called the Pupa Stage or the transition stage. The caterpillar goes into hiding. Anytime you go into hiding, this is the perfect environment for transformation. When a cake goes into the oven, it transforms. David, in the Bible, went into the cave. Jesus went into the tomb. A butterfly goes into the cocoon. I had been avoiding being alone with myself so that I did not have to feel the pain that I had been pushing farther and farther down.

The tomb and the cocoon possess many similarities. They are both dark, lonely places. If you will acquiesce to the cocoon; surrender to the call to be alone with yourself, a transformation will take place. Your ashes will be turned into beauty.

When you are being compelled into the cocoon, sometimes you've just gotta let ugly happen. Surrendering to that dark, lonely place of development is the best option. It is all a part of the process. I heard someone say, "This too, shall pass...it may pass like a kidney stone, but it shall pass." (Author unknown) Getting comfortable with being uncomfortable is the nature of this phase of development.

What Happens in the Cocoon Stays in the Cocoon

As the caterpillar prepares to enter the cocoon, she spins it herself. It is something that she intuitively does using the silk thread that is within her. Saying yes to the cocoon in *The Cave* phase of development is instinctive to your rise. It is a journey that must be forged on your own. Everything you need for this season of metamorphosis is within you. You do not need anything outside of yourself. You do not need permission from anyone else. You do not need validation from others. You do not even need the approval of others in order to make it through what is about to happen in the cocoon.

2 Peter 1:3 says, "For His divine power has bestowed on us [absolutely] everything necessary for [a dynamic spiritual] life and godliness, through true and personal knowledge of Him who called us by His own glory and excellence." AMP

Absolutely everything you need is inside of you and available to you to endure the dark, lonely cave experience as you are wrapped up in the protection of the cocoon. The cocoon, with its silk inner-lining and hard outer-shell, becomes the encasing for the grace-lined fortification where the deconstruction and the reconstruction of whom you were created to be can unfold.

The DNA of Greatness is Within You

Once the caterpillar is tucked safely away in the cocoon she stops eating and becomes a chrysalis. A caterpillar can lose up to half of its weight during this time. Once you are nestled away in your cocoon of development, often times you will experience loss, but a loss is not a sign of rejection or denial. In this season of life, the loss becomes an indicator that you are in the right place at the right time and perfectly positioned for true transformation to take place.

You have to be willing to let go of the former identity that you created – a mere shell of the woman that you are meant to become in order to embrace your new identity of a butterfly. As I mentioned in a previous chapter, the DNA of a butterfly is wrapped up inside of the caterpillar. As a caterpillar eats and moseys through life, she is not trying to become something different; she is compelled to transform into who she really is. The body of a caterpillar is just the container for the most authentic version of whom she was originally created to be. The DNA of the most authentic version is inside of you and it is longing to be transformed into a vessel that is capable of rising to new heights.

That secret longing for an extraordinary life of significance, fulfillment and true joy is real. That is your original DNA of greatness that is yearning to emerge out of you. Mindsets of lack and "I am not enough" squelch our rise. You do not have to feel guilty for wanting a bigger life. We are conditioned to believe that wanting to be seen and heard is self-serving or prideful, but it is not. You are destined to be visible and vocal. You were constructed and created with seeds of greatness. It is not just in some of us but it is in all of us. You have the answer to someone's question. You have the healing to someone's wound. You carry within you the solution to someone's problem. If you stay hidden and underdeveloped, you are not the only one who suffers. Your rise impacts generations to come.

As the Borg Would Say, "Resistance is Futile"

As the caterpillar is now situated in the cocoon, she can no longer excrete. She loses the ability to eliminate her own waste. She is stuck in the cocoon with her own crap, excuse my language here. This is exactly what happens when you are in your dark, lonely cocoon of transformation. You come face to face with your perception of the past, your negative emotions and the old mindsets that have kept you stuck and spinning your wheels. In the cocoon is where the deadly cycle of disappointment, disillusionment, and distraction is broken, but first, you must be confronted with it. What may seem detrimental to your development becomes necessary for your advancement. At this stage of development, avoidance is no longer a viable option. What you resist will persist. The Borg, in Star Trek, the Next Generation touted to the Starship Enterprise captain, "Resistance is futile! You will be assimilated!"

Resistance in the cocoon of *The Cave* phase of development will render you fruitless and stuck there for longer than necessary. This is a great time to do as the old saying goes, "Let go and let God!"

The Power of the Deep

One of my favorite songs is by Hillsong United called, "Oceans (Where Feet May Fail.)"

The lyrics say,

> *"You call me out upon the waters; the great unknown where feet may fail. And there I find You in the mystery in oceans deep my faith will stand."*[15]

I have sung that song at the top of my lungs giving God the OK to take me out into the deep – a place where I no longer have the stability of the dry ground to keep me comfortable. Sometimes once you get out in the deep, you look around and second guess your bold request to go where faith is your only hope.

The deep is just like *The Cave*. It brings the unknown and the unknown is scary. What you know and what you can be assured of feels so much safer. Not everyone is called to be a sailor out on the open waters, but when you know that the deep is calling you, you will not be satisfied anywhere else.

Ships sail in deep waters. Ships have buoyancy; they have the ability to float. Faith is that buoyancy that keeps us afloat in the midst of the deep. When the sails are hoisted, ships are powered by the wind. Ships are guided by the celestial. Sailors keep their eyes on the sky for their direction. You are called to be led by the wind of the Spirit. If you look down at your surroundings you may feel lost and hopeless.

To all of my sailor friends who are called to be out in the open waters where faith demands total reliance on God, remember that He created you to glide across the deep even though you float upon the unknown. Being in the cocoon, *The Cave* is an opportunity to go deep. It is a time to jump into what you have been avoiding and make it your new swimming pool. The deep is calling you.

Silk-Lined

The cocoon is lined with silk. Silk is soft and comforting. It is actually luxurious by nature. I find it so interesting that the dark and lonely encasement of the cocoon is coated with a comforting, luxurious silk that makes the metamorphosis bearable. Graces surrounds us in our dark and lonely vessel of renovation and eases the growing pains. Even though transformation can be painful, there is a reassuring element that keeps you comfortable so that you can endure the whole process.

Pupa Soup

Once the caterpillar has spun her cocoon she rests gently in the caress of the silk-lined container. She has lost half of her weight and is swimming in the murky waters of her own waste and then enzymes are released throughout the cocoon. These enzymes begin to breakdown the tissue of the caterpillar, leaving only the cells that will eventually regroup into eyes, legs, and wings.[16]

You will know you are in the cocoon if what once has structure and form now resembles a formless blob. For me, nothing in my life looked the way it once did. I was in completely unfamiliar territory. I was unacquainted with this life of solitude. There was nothing conversant about the way things had turned out. I had gone from a big home, surrounded by lots of children and loved ones, impacting people's lives through our ministry, never having to worry about money or bills to living alone, being the sole provider for my family and working a job that had no connection to my purpose.

I remember conversing with "The Karen's" about my dire financial situation. Upon their recommendation, I swallowed my pride and stood in the food stamp line. If you had told me a year earlier that this foodie would have been cheffin' up delicacies purchased with food stamps, I never would have believed you. Nevertheless, that is where I found myself. Just to prove the point of how drastically my life had morphed into something unrecognizable, as I was in line preparing the paperwork to request government assistance, I looked down at my wrist and realized I was standing in the food stamp line wearing a Rolex watch with diamonds. Even if no one else noticed, I am sure my face went red and my eyes got as big as saucers as I stood gripped with the reminder of the devastating events that had just taken place in my life.

You see, after my divorce, I had sold all of my jewelry to help make ends meet, but when it came to my Rolex, I had not found anyone to pay me a substantial amount for it. I continued to wear it as an advertisement that it was for sale. In the meantime, I inadvertently wore it in the wrong place at the wrong time. Had the counselor seen that, I am sure I would have been denied the help. I quickly whisked the watch off my wrist and threw it in my purse just in the nick of time. The rest of the story is that a few weeks later, I walked into a jewelry store that bought used Rolex watches. To my surprise, there stood a dear friend who had just started working at that establishment. He spoke to the owner and made sure I got a fair price for my watch. I sold my Rolex that day and used some of the money to buy my kids Christmas gifts.

I was living in the dark night of my soul. Who I once was had completely melted away into an unrecognizable life in the cocoon. The process of breaking down the former structure that embodied the caterpillar is a necessary component in the development of the butterfly and cannot be forgone.

Somehow, I felt safe in the confinement of conversion. Something instinctual reassured me that this was part of the process. I knew this was not a season that I wanted to exit too early. I was committed to extracting every ounce of wisdom and knowledge out of that season as possible so that I did not have to go back a second time. Acquiescing to this part of the process, releasing your past and truly letting go of what was, is the only way you can be open to understanding *The Call.*

Chapter 9

The Call

"God never wastes a hurt." Richard Foster

Merriam-Webster dictionary defines "calling" as, "a strong inner impulse toward a particular course of action especially when accompanied by conviction of divine influence."17

The Call is your summons to soar; it beckons you to fly higher than you have ever been before. It is a divine directive that gives your life meaning and purpose. It is the question you are here to answer and the hurt you are here to heal. It is the story you are here to tell and the message of hope that you are here to herald. *The Call* is a spiritual endowment. It is your divine assignment and your job is to come into alignment with it so that you will be authorized to make the impact on this earth that only you can make. *The Call* is your life as a butterfly.

The Call begins with a stirring, a dream of making the world a better place. It is a holy dissatisfaction about the way things are and a desire to do something about it. This discontentment is different from disappointment about the way things have turned out. *The Call* is where the diamonds of your story, along with your mission, vision, purpose, values, passion and potential culminate into the specific job that you were created to do.

When you have spent most of your days as a caterpillar, inching your way through life with a limited vision for anything past what is in front of you, it is easy to lose sight of the impact that you are destined for. Inside of the cocoon is where that vision is stirred once again. Once you have come face to face with the pain of your past, you can reframe the painful events of your past as the perfect preparation for what lies ahead. Feeling the stir of your call in the cocoon stimulates hope and expectation. It lets you know that none of what you are going through is in vain. It becomes a reminder that there is a purpose in the pain of your past and provision for the inner renovation that is taking place.

You have most likely felt the stirring of your call since you were a young child but somewhere along the way, it gets covered up by thoughts of "I am not good enough," "who am I to think that I can make a difference?" or "it is too late for me." You allow your past to define you as broken or unworthy, but that is not true. You are not broken. You only need to be more effective. Just like the caterpillar who has the DNA of a butterfly, your call was deposited inside of you before you were in your mother's womb. You have everything you need inside of you to align all of your gifts and talents along with who you are at your core and accomplish the task that you were given.

Why Clarity About *The Call* Matters

The Call **marks you.** It is like the colors on the butterfly's wings. The coloration of a butterfly's wings allows it to camouflage, connect with other butterflies or warn predators of its poisonous essence.[18] Your call will divulge important information about who you are and what you stand for without a spoken word. *The Call* is an unspoken declaration that connects you with your purpose.

The Call reveals your sphere of influence and connects you to your community. It becomes a clarion call to the right people and assists you in repelling the ones who are not a part of your tribe. In the book by Jim Collins, *Going from Good to Great*, he talks about getting the right people on the bus and leaving some people at the bus stop.

> *"In fact, leaders of companies that go from good to great start not with "where" but with "who." They start by getting the right people on the bus, the wrong people off the bus, and the right people in the right seats."*

When you connect with your call, you no longer feel guilty when removing toxic people from your bus. Commitment to *The Call* wakes up an obligation to focus and intention. You begin to realize that it is imperative to feel the weight of responsibility that accompanies your call above the weight of hurting someone's feelings.

The Call reveals your path. Once you recognize and determine your call, then your call lets you know how to move forward. It directs you and lights the path. Along the path, *The Call* opens doors of opportunity that align with your purpose and closes doors that do not align. *The Call* becomes a plumb line to measure strategic action by. It casts a shadow on trivial tasks and focuses you on what is vital. When *The Call* is stirred once again, inconsequential mindsets melt away; mindsets like the need for approval or outside validation, people-pleasing, procrastination or being a control-freak. Your face is set like flint and little can distract you.

***The Call* consecrates you.** It sets you apart for special use. When you are in alignment with your call it makes your journey sacred. It sets you up for supernatural encounters where heaven partners with you to accomplish your special mission. As *The Call* consecrates you, it stirs a devotion inside of you that commands a forward gaze. Precision becomes a result of focusing on a mission that compels you, rather than the effects of willpower in pursuit of perfection. When you focus on *The Call*, anything that would distract from your purpose loses the enticement that it once had. You live a life that is set apart for special use, unencumbered by useless impropriety.

When you commit to *The Call* it is as if you were a marksman hitting the bullseye. If you know you have a bullseye to hit and you are being a poor marksman, this is when you beat yourself up. Hitting the outer rims of the target does not bring the same satisfaction as hitting the center of the bullseye dead on.

If you grew up in a religious home, the idea of sin and repentance may bring an image to your mind of self-loathing, crawl-to-the-altar to be absolved of your sins type picture. It may stir memories of sitting heavy-laden with guilt in a confessional booth. Sins can include a wide range of activities from drinking or drugs to lust or sex outside of marriage and a lot of things in-between. Not that I am advocating any of these activities, but my point is that the meaning of the word "sin" in Greek, which is one of the original languages that the Bible was written in, is the word *harmatia*, meaning "to miss the mark."[19] The Greek word for "repentance" is *metanoia* which means "to change one's mind."[20] In the Jewish tradition, repentance was represented as *Teshuvah* which means "a returning." It was a word that depicted a person walking in one direction but had a change of mind, turned around and walked in the opposite direction.[21]

When you tie the original meaning of "sin" with the meaning of "repentance" you have the word picture of a marksman with a bow and arrow. Instead of aiming at the target, he has completely turned around, facing in the opposite direction of the target. You can be participating in sin when you are missing the mark of your existence – when you are aiming at anything other than *The Call*.

Before you cast a shadow of judgment upon the poor souls who participate in lasciviousness and lude behavior, consider the areas where you are missing the mark of your own purpose for which you were created. Where have you been aiming in a direction other than towards the bullseye of your original design? The exciting news is that if you have been misdirected in regards to your call, all you have to do is to turn around and walk in the opposite direction. Focus on the center of the bullseye, pull back the shaft of the arrow and release the bow. True repentance requires a change in mindset which leads to a change in behavior.

While you are wrapped up in the cocoon, *The Call* is reactivated so that you have a glimpse of what your future holds. Even though your calling and purpose are constrained within the confines of development, it is imperative that it is reawakened inside of you at this juncture. Activation and opportunities to step into *The Call* will come later in *The Debut* phase of life.

Preparation for the Palace

> *Esther 2: 8-11 says, "8 So it came about when the command and decree of the king were heard and many young ladies were gathered to the citadel of Susa into the custody of Hegai, that Esther was taken to the king's [a]palace into the custody of Hegai, who was in charge of the women. 9 Now the young lady pleased him and found favor with him. So he quickly provided her with her cosmetics and [b]food, gave her seven choice maids from the*

> *king's palace and transferred her and her maids to the best place in the harem. 10 Esther did not make known her people or her kindred, for Mordecai had instructed her that she should not make them known. 11 Every day Mordecai walked back and forth in front of the court of the harem to learn how Esther was and how she fared." AMP*

Recognizing *The Call* and waking up to your full potential is what prepares you for the palace. As you follow the Biblical story of Hadassah, who would be renamed Esther; she was swept away from her normal surroundings into a place of preparation, cared for by a eunuch named Hegai. I can only imagine that as she was provided with cosmetics and seven maids to care for her that it had to have caused a mind shift in her. I am sure that she began to see herself differently. She must have seen herself transforming from being that little orphan girl to beginning to see herself as having the ability to be the queen one day.

The Call to become the queen began to surface inside of her before she ever made it to the palace. That same call allowed her to find favor and connect with the right people as it shined the light on her path to the palace. This process is known as *The Becoming*. *The Becoming* stage of development is the third phase that every woman has the opportunity to walk through. In the following chapters, we will discuss *The Becoming* which is the process of becoming a butterfly inside of the cocoon after the caterpillar has been dissolved.

Phase Three

The Becoming

Angela Aja

Chapter 10

The Becoming

"Life is a lively process of becoming." Douglas Mac Arthur

The Becoming is the third phase of development that every woman has the opportunity to pass through before she begins to see her wings form. *The Becoming* is a continuation of what has been happening inside of the cocoon. We will discuss the inner workings of the metamorphosis that is taking place inside of the cocoon in the pages ahead, but as for now, rest assured that this hidden season of development is all a part of a grand design.

The word "become" means to be developed into or the converting of something into another thing.[22] *The Becoming* phase of life is all about change. Change begins to show up as deep transformation. Transformation is the altering of something in one state into another state of being. When a woman is going through a process of becoming, she has to let go of the woman that she has become in order to step into the fullness of the woman that she was created to be.

When a woman is entering into *The Becoming* phase, life may take on a completely new form and fashion. In many cases, life feels like it has been turned upside down and everything that was once familiar turns into unfamiliar. A woman in this phase may have been thrust into a season of feeling stuck and spinning her wheels, but it is for the purpose of remodeling and re-designing a life of intention.

Awakening to Your Authenticity

A woman in *The Becoming* stage of development is no longer afraid to face her greatest fears and disappointments. She is ready to view the woman in the mirror and see what is really going on as opposed to the fantasy of perfection. A woman who is in *The Becoming* stage of development has felt the wooing to pull away from the crowds; to enter a season of seclusion. She needs to be alone with herself and her Maker to understand who He created her to be instead of who she has been masquerading around as. She is ready to subdue the fear loneliness so she can learn to appreciate alone-time and deep reflection.

She is beginning to awaken to her authenticity. Her truest identity is being revealed – who she is at her core. She begins to become aware of the masks of self-preservation that she has worn; fear, disappointment, regret, shame, blame, and guilt; morphing into a false version of whom she was created to be. These are all symptoms that propel her into a lifestyle of hiding and playing small - but symptoms can't mask true purpose. Even in her feelings of desperation and despair, there is a sense that nothing she is experiencing is in vain. She can sense the essence of transformation at work down in the depths of her soul.

This is a time when a woman reflects inwardly on herself – I am not talking about a selfish, narcissistic, inward-focused. The word "selfish" means to be preoccupied with one's self and one's own affairs[23], but the meaning of the word "self-love" is regard for one's own well-being and happiness.[24] Excessive inward focus is narcissism, but narcissism is nothing more than an overcompensation attempt at an intense lack of self-love. (...and a narcissist cannot be a narcissist without a codependent counterpart...but that is another discussion for another day!) Taking some time to inwardly reflect on your own well-being lays a sturdy foundation on which to build. This is where I find that most women suffer from severe self-neglect.

Remember when we talked about the instructions of the stewardess on the plane? Even though it sounds counter-intuitive, she clearly instructs you to put the mask on yourself first – even if you are sitting next to a small child or someone who needs your help. Wow! The reason behind these instructions is that if you run out of oxygen, you and the person sitting next to you will both lose out. If you put the mask on yourself first, then you will be invigorated and able to help others. When you put the *mask on yourself* during this season of personal development and take time to breathe, then you will be able to give out of an abundance rather than out of a depleted state. This creates a win/win scenario!

Women are nurturers by nature. They give and give, yet neglect themselves. Women often tell me that they are last on the list. They report that they do not have enough time to consider themselves because they are so busy caring for everyone else around them. The problem is that when you do not take the time to be replenished – to consider yourself, then you give out of a depleted state and everyone comes up empty. But, when you say "YES" to your hidden times of development and consider the state of your own affairs, then you will be able to sustain the weight of caring for yourself and others while giving from a place of abundance.

Forget About It! (In a New York Accent...)

During *The Becoming* phase, there is a supernatural peace that resides on the inside of this evolving woman that brings a calmness and trust as she goes through the full process of development. There is a new sense of emotional resilience that pulses through her veins. She begins to understand that it is not what happened to her that has caused her suffering, but the old story that she told herself about what happened. She is becoming aware that she can rewrite her story as the hero and mine the diamonds of her past that she had only seen as lumps of coal. She is beginning to recognize that everything she has overcome was laid out with purposeful design. She is awakening to the realization that her ashes can be repurposed into something beautiful. It is becoming apparent that God is working all things out together for her good.

> *Romans 8:28 says it perfectly, "And we know [with great confidence] that God [who is deeply concerned about us] causes all things to work together [as a plan] for good for those who love God, to those who are called according to His plan and purpose."*

This is a season for her to embody the following verse:

> *Philippians 3:13b "Forgetting what lies behind, I press on toward the goal of the upward call of God in Christ Jesus." AMP*

For anyone who has been victimized or harmed in any way, I am in no way suggesting the idea that you should just forget about it and get over it. There are times when being the victim is an appropriate response. If you have been the victim of a crime or abuse, it is important to take the necessary actions to find protection, help, and healing. However, after the recovery from victimization has occurred, it is suitable to lay down the label of *victim*. When you allow what happened to you to label you or become your identity then you go from being the victim of what happened to staying the victim in life. It is from this foundation that I am suggesting that reframing the events of your past might make you more effective in accomplishing your purpose.

There are also times when you tell yourself that you are a victim to something or someone that has no power over you. You decide that something outside of you has control over you. Whatever you hand your power over to is what you become a victim to. If you retain the power through responsibility, accountability and owning your contribution then you remain in control. You are not a victim to your past. You are not powerless over your past. You have influence over your past by choosing the meaning that it has in your life.

Here is my example of how I changed the story I was telling myself about what happened to me:

I went through a devastating divorce, financial hardship, betrayal, and abandonment. I spent many years anguishing over the events in my past, but when I shifted my perspective about what happened, then I was able to find the beauty from my ashes. I rewrote the story that I was unlovable, not worth keeping, less than, not good enough, not pretty enough, blah, blah, blah (you get the picture) to I am worth loving, I deserve to be respected and treated properly, I can be cherished and adored. I own my contribution to the breakdown of my marriage and I recognize that I had built my identity around a man and the ministry. I morphed into a false version of whom I was created to be which left me vulnerable to mental and emotional abuse. My resilience laid the foundation for forgiveness, inner-healing, and self-love which opened up the door for me to use my story to inspire others toward the same results. Even though I was victimized, I am no longer a victim to the experiences of my life. They do not define me. I went from victim to victor by scripting a new narrative about the events of my life.

I was able to do what Paul instructs us to do and forget the former things so that I could realize a greater purpose out of my pain. You would not be reading this book today had I not gone through the devastating events that I had the privilege of experiencing. In order to make that shift, I had to reframe my memories about what happened.

Think about this mind-bending question...what if your past was not real – what if it was only the memories that you have framed in your mind about what happened. The reason that this is such an opportunity for freedom is that if your past isn't real – if it's just your perception about what's real, then by shifting your perspective, you can literally change the impact that your past has had on you.

Let me explain...

About 20 years ago, there was a bank robbery with hostages taken. Thankfully, after several hours of being held at gunpoint, the victims were released unharmed. A psychologist contacted all of the previous hostages and asked them to write their story while it was fresh in their mind. Ten years later, the psychologist contacted them again and, once again asked them to rewrite the story of what happened that day when they had been held hostage. What she discovered was that the story they had written the day of the event was nothing like what they wrote ten years later. When she handed them back the stories that they had written the day of the event, some of them denied that they had written it. They insisted that someone had gone and changed their story. With time, their memories of the events of that dreadful day had completely shifted into another story.

> *"A memory is not simply an image produced by time traveling back to the original event – it can be an image that is somewhat distorted because of the prior times you remembered it,* "said Donna Bridge, a postdoctoral fellow at Northwestern University Feinburg School of Medicine and lead author *"Memories aren't static. If you remember something in the context of a new environment and time, or if you are even in a different mood, your memories might integrate new information."*[25]

This is just a technical way to say that the past is not reality. Your past is the conglomeration of cognitive perception that you attach a certain meaning to.

For example, freedom from your past happens when you grant yourself permission to see your story from a fresh perspective. It is permission to live again, to move forward and walk out your purpose with a grand design. A few years ago, I was driving back to Austin from Houston and my car broke down on the side of the road. I had my car towed to a nearby town and later that week, I received a call that my car was repaired and was ready to be picked up. My car was about two hours away from Houston. I had tried to arranged for a friend to drive me to my car to no avail. My only option was to have Austin, my 19-year-old son, take me to my car. My friend had loaned me her car so that Austin and I could drive there together and then he would drive my car home while I would drive my friend's car home. The plan was working like a well-oiled machine...that is, until we arrived at the mechanic's place of business. As we were getting in separate cars, it started pouring rain. To top it off, Austin, my son who is nearly blind, had left his glasses at work and now had the task of driving my car, visually impaired, in monsoon-like conditions and it was now getting dark.

We decided to move forward with our plan. Austin followed closely behind me as we both drove like two little old grandmas on a Sunday drive. The stress was mounting by the minute. We finally made it to our exit where we would be able to get off of the interstate and onto the back-country roads. Just as I took a big sigh of relief, I looked in my rear-view mirror to see a big 18-wheeler behind Austin, barreling in on us. Being on a two-way highway, passing conditions were treacherous at best. The truck relentlessly stayed on our tale. I kept looking back in my rear-view mirror to make sure Austin was still in my sight. The pressure of this monstrosity in my rear-view mirror was overwhelming. To make matters worse, the truck was not just in my rear-view mirror, but in Austin's rearview mirror, too.

We made it home and all was well. We survived the trip from hell. As I lay in bed that night, recounting the events of the day, I had a huge revelation. That truck was just like my past. It had been barreling in on me, causing me so much stress. It kept my focus in my rear-view mirror. Not only was it in hot pursuit of me, but my kids as well. My past had been tormenting me, taunting me with thoughts of fear, loss, and defeat. All of a sudden, I had an "aha moment." I pictured that truck, lying on its side and me standing on top of it! I thought to myself, it is now time to let my past become my platform. I pictured myself standing on top of the very thing that had kept me looking backward for so long. That day, I stepped into freedom from my past.

It is not the specific tragedies, abuses or hurtful events that happen to you that cause your long-term suffering, but rather the story you tell yourself, over the course of your life, about what happened to you. It is time to script a new narrative; it is time to mine for diamonds. During this season of *The Becoming*, it is imperative to forget about your past, lay down the old story of fear, disappointment, regret, shame, blame and guilt that you have been telling yourself and embrace a new meaning to all that you have been through.

Becoming Your Own Best Advocate

It is important, at this stage to comprehend the dynamic results of keeping your word. As I coach women, one thing I often hear is they do not trust themselves. If you are not in the habit of keeping your word to yourself, you subconsciously know that your word is not trustworthy. Therefore, when you speak, nothing happens. The more you practice keeping your word and trusting yourself, the more power your words will have.

When a woman is smack dab in the middle of *The Becoming* she begins to comprehend the power of her "YES" and her "NO." When you begin to awaken to your authenticity, you can be led by your mission, vision, and purpose rather than driven by the demands of others. You will no longer say "YES" as a people-pleaser, perfectionist or a control-freak. As you awaken to your authenticity, you will only say "YES" to the things that are in alignment with who you are at your core and what you want. You will say "NO" without feeling guilty and you will be able to hear "NO" without feeling rejection.

One of my clients, whom we will call "Becky" told me early on in our coaching sessions that she had a hard time saying "NO," so she said "YES" to anything and everything. She was feeling completely exhausted, overwhelmed and resentful because she felt taken advantage of. As we went through the program, I shared with Becky a very important coaching principle, "Your **why** is always more important than your **what**."

Let me explain it like this if you were walking down the street with a young child and you came up to a street light and as you were waiting to cross the street, you reach over and shove that child to the ground...are you a mean person? The answer to that question is in the **why**. If you pushed the child down for no reason, then yes, you might be considered to be a mean person. However, if you shoved the child to the ground because you saw an out-of-control car heading right for the child and you shoved her out of the way of the reckless vehicle, then you might be considered a hero. Your **why** is more important than your **what**.

> *Matthew 5:37 Amplified Bible says, "But let your statement be, 'Yes, yes' or 'No, no' [a firm yes or no]; anything more than that comes from the evil one." AMP*

When you say "YES" but you mean "NO," or when you say "NO" when you mean "YES," then you are robbed of the benefits of your good deeds and you are training your own mind that your word does not carry any weight at all. This concept is crucial in *The Becoming* phase as it prepares you for your queenly authority in *The Rise*.

> *Job 22:28 says, "You will also decree a thing, and it will be established for you." KJV*

If you cannot trust yourself to keep your word to yourself, you will not trust yourself to decree something and see it come to pass. Practicing the art of keeping your word to yourself in this season prepares you for decreeing a thing in the seasons to come. If you have been decreeing things and they are not coming to pass, do an internal audit. Investigate areas that you may not be keeping your word to yourself. If your subconscious mind is trained that you mean business when you speak, then your declaration will shift your circumstances.

I often hear from women that they have trust issues. I would like to boldly say that if you have trust issues, the problem is not that you do not trust other people, but that you do not trust yourself. Trust yourself when you have that gut feeling. Trust yourself to be discerning. Trust yourself to make *good* decisions and if it turns out to be a *bad* decision, trust yourself to get back on track easily and effortlessly while learning from your mistakes.

Allied with Yourself and Your Surroundings

Many women have reported to me that they constantly beat themselves up. They are their own worst enemy. However, during *The Becoming* phase of life, a woman becomes allied with herself and her surroundings. She is beginning to express self-love and self-compassion, honoring herself as a creation of the God. Not only is she beginning to walk in forgiveness for anyone who has hurt her in her past, but she is extending self-forgiveness. She is releasing herself from the guilt and shame of whom she was *supposed to be* or what she was *supposed to do*: the mistakes and missteps that she has made along the way. She extends a new level of grace to herself and is allowing herself to trust her inner-nudging's. She is beginning to trust her gut and listen to her intuition – the inner guidance of the Holy Spirit.

This is absolutely necessary in preparation for what is to come. You will not be able to withstand the happenings of *The Debut* if you are still carrying the heavy load of blame, shame or guilt. As you will see in the next chapter, everything you have been through was in preparation for your rise!

You Can Stop Apologizing Now

Where does the need to apologize for the light inside of us come from? Why do women feel more comfortable diminishing their value than standing in the greatness that God placed in the vessel that contains the glory of God?

In *The Becoming* phase of a woman's journey is when she can stop apologizing for who she is and what she feels called to do.

One of my greatest breakthroughs came when I realized that there was nothing wrong with me. My life began to change for the better when I stopped apologizing for my strengths and acting contrite for the big dreams that God had placed inside of me.

I recently worked with a woman who was in the habit of diminishing herself. Part of the process that I take women through is to take a personality test. She studied her strengths and her weaknesses, which every person has. As she began to peel back the layers of her own nature and temperament, she had some major *aha moments* about herself and I could see confidence stirring inside of her. Recognizing her strengths, she was able to see the value that she brought to the world. But, as we talked about her weaknesses, she began apologizing for the parts of her personality that she deemed as undesirable. So, I had her make a list of all of her *perceived weaknesses*. As she looked over her list, she held her head down low with shame and guilt. "I need to fix these weaknesses!" she touted. I then instructed her to go down her list of weaknesses and ask the same question of each one, "What's great about this?"

While it was a struggle at first, she found ways that weaknesses were a huge blessing to her family. She reframed her *weakness* as *uniqueness* that she brought as gifts to the world.

I do not believe that there is anything wrong with you. You are not broken and you do not need to be fixed. You only need to be more effective. Reframing your weaknesses as unique gifts will help you stop apologizing, hiding and playing small.

I worked with a young missionary – a woman who had dedicated her life to serving God and serving others. Throughout our twelve weeks together, I would ask her the question, "What value do you bring to the world?" Even in her life of dedication to God, she had grown accustomed to devaluing the magnitude of her surrendered service. She had become completely blinded to the worth of her selfless devotion to humanity. Somehow, she felt that it was more spiritual to devalue the work that she did. As time went on, she began to grow more comfortable with stating the value of her gifts and talents. This led to open doors and opportunities that she had no idea were available to her. This built a new foundation from which she was able to reach more people in less time – all because she stopped apologizing for her selfless acts of service.

The word "sorry" means "pitiful."[26] When a woman continually says "I'm sorry," she is releasing a self-fulfilling prophecy about her own pitiful state. You cannot rise up into the fullness of whom you were created to be by declaring how pitiful you are. That serves no one!

It is time to stop apologizing for the wonderous version of whom God created you to be. Even your weaknesses add value to the world around you.

Emotional Responsibility

A woman in the middle of *The Becoming* phase is beginning to own a sense of emotional responsibility, as she is released from victimhood. Even if she was victimized in her past, she begins to lay down the victim mask and take responsibility for her own actions, thoughts, patterns, and behaviors. She begins to grasp that she can be her own best advocate. She can practice self-care without guilt. She is beginning to affirm herself, no longer looking outside of herself for validation and approval.

She is realizing that her voice matters. No longer can she stay hidden and small. No longer can she settle for a life of insignificance. Her time of ignoring the gifts that God has placed in her is over. She was born to soar and the voice of who she is resounds; it is getting louder as if to silence the voice of whom she has turned into.

A woman who is in *The Becoming* phase of life is awakening to her Divine assignment. That call to impact the world in a bigger way, that she has sensed deep within since she was a little girl, is stirring once again. She is beginning to dream again. She is getting comfortable with the idea of being uncomfortable; stepping out of her comfort zone into the realm of possibility. Even in the midst of this season of isolation, excitement for a life of significance, fulfillment and true joy is rising up from impossible to a real possibility.

The cultivation that takes place in *The Becoming* is a one-woman job. This is a road that must be walked alone. This is not a journey that can be taken as a group. Relationships change during this phase. Allowing relationships to shift without guilt is essential in this phase of development. Just because someone had access to you in one season of your life does not mean that they automatically have the same access to you as you rise. It is all right to make choices about your relationships that will support you in your season of metamorphosis.

I have heard women say things like, "I feel like I am being a bad friend if I do not sit and let her dump all of her problems on me." I have also heard, "I feel so guilty not hanging out with her even though I am completely drained after I have spent time with her". You are responsible for protecting your energy. If you will concentrate your energies inwardly during this season, you will have more to give in the days ahead. The conservation of your energy in this phase is absolutely necessary for the radical transformations that are taking place.

The Becoming takes time. It is an inescapable process that must occur. It cannot be cheated; it cannot be skipped over with short-cuts and side-winders. It is a road paved directly down the middle of death to the old and being resurrected into a more authentic version of whom you were created to be. It is a journey into the dark night of your soul; a baptism in brutal self-reflection and gut-piercing honesty. It takes grit and commitment that not everyone can endure. That is why so many slips back into the previous phase, stuck on the hamster wheel of *The Ordinary*. Not everyone can tolerate the transformational process. It is no wonder why our subconscious kicks and screams, throwing childlike tantrums. It throws up smoke and mirrors to hoodwink us into avoidance of the metamorphosis that our soul is compelling us to surrender to.

> *Romans 12:2 says, "Do not conform to the pattern of this world, but be transformed by the renewing of your mind. Then you will be able to test and approve what God's will is—his good, pleasing and perfect will. NIV*

I remember *The Becoming* phase of my life as if it were yesterday. I had moved to a new city where I knew very few people. I felt secluded and isolated yet, safe and secure. I was tucked away in the confines of my new residence, with a new job and no social circle. I felt so alone, yet somehow, I knew I was exactly where I was supposed to be. My past was still so prevalent and memories of my failures and disappointments still haunted me. The ghosts of my former life seemed to be clinging on to me as if they somehow knew that their days were numbered. Old thoughts of victimization and abandonment screamed in my ear. Old patterns of hiding and being obscure kept me chained to a pole like a baby circus elephant. Fearful thoughts of being unwanted and unlovable taunted me with evil laughter as if to say, "You will never be loved again!" "You are not worth being loved or cared for," and "Your marriage failed – you are a failure!" Finally, after months of wallowing in self-pity, I suited up for battle. I knew it was time to die to my expectations of staying stuck and being happy at the same time. I acquiesced to *The Becoming*.

> *Isaiah 43: 18-19 says, "God says - Forget about what happened; don't keep going over old history. Be alert. Be present. I'm about to do something brand-new. I'm bursting out. Don't you see it?" MSG*

This season will not last forever! There will come a time when preparation meets the fullness of time and everything will begin to come together, but as for now, the breakdown is necessary for the breakthrough to take place.

Chapter 11

The Metamorphosis

"How does one become a butterfly?" Pooh asked pensively. "You must want to fly so much that you are willing to give up being a caterpillar," Piglet replied. "You mean die?" asked Pooh. "Yes and no," he answered. "What looks like you will die, REALLY you will live on." A.A. Milne

The Breakdown is Necessary for the Breakthrough

At this point, there is so much going on under the surface of the hard, outer shell of the cocoon. What is unseen far outweighs what is seen. The caterpillar has completely dissolved and the cells enter a state of resurgence as they regroup and reform into the shape of something new – a butterfly. The destruction of the former is complete and the caterpillar has dissolved into an unrecognizable shapeless substance. The breakdown is necessary for the breakthrough. This phase is where noticeable changes are beginning to take place. A reorganization of cells displays themselves as multi-faceted eyes, antennae, wings, and longer legs. *The Becoming* involves a metamorphosis that shows up in the form of a reformation.

Just as I mentioned before, the cocoon is lined with silk, this is a season of grace for the woman who is wrapped up in the middle of a transformation. There is a softness within the dark, lonely place of confinement that makes an uncomfortable place as comfortable as possible. Self-compassion is a necessity in the middle of *The Metamorphosis*.

What is Really Going on in There?

Once the collapse of the former is complete, the new can now come together.

As for you, when you are in your cocoon, after the breakdowns, after facing your old mindsets, after saying YES to a season of lonely reflection, this is where you step into the reformation of who you were always been meant to be. The real you begins to take shape.

The metamorphosis that is taking place in *The Becoming* is a process of identity development. It is an identity makeover, so to speak. This is where you discover your mission, vision, purpose, values, passion, and potential. Just like the butterfly, you are going through a process of resurgence, a divine renaissance, if you will. During the metamorphosis of *The Becoming* phase, you are literally being reinvented. However, you are not trying to become something you are not, but rather you are releasing the most authentic version of who you are.

Upside-down and Inside-out

The cocoon hangs upside down during the metamorphosis process. If you feel like life has been turned upside down, you are perfectly positioned for metamorphosis to take place. Hanging upside down, the cocoon is positioned in such a way that allows nature to defy gravity. Proper placement is imperative during the phase of *The Becoming*. This upside-down vantage point shifts your perspective so that you can see things you may have been unwilling to look at before. You see things from a completely new viewpoint.

Remember that the cocoon is dark and lonely. It is an inside job that will eventually produce outward results, but not before the full process of transformation has taken place. Everything you ate as a caterpillar is now being used as fuel for your transformation.

Enzymes are released inside of the cocoon that breakdown the former structure of the caterpillar and turn her into "pupa soup." The foundations that you have built your life on become null and void. I remember this season of my life well! I had built my entire identity around a man and the ministry. When both of those disintegrated into nothingness, I suffered from an intense identity crisis. I had built an identity around what I did versus who I am at my core. Just like the little caterpillar, alone in the cocoon, I felt like I was going to drown in the pool of my own tears. Little did I know that I was right on track. What I could not see at the time was that I was not going to drown in my sorrows. The life that I had created had to be liquified so that it could melt away; my old life had to be dissolved so that the Master Creator could reshape me into a more effective vessel.

All that is left after the breakdown are the imaginal discs, also called "sleeping cells."[27] The imaginal discs are the building blocks for the reformation to begin. They are a highly organized group of cells that survive the digestive process and form into the adult body parts.[28] Everything the caterpillar needs to become a butterfly is already within her.

> 2 Peter 1:3 says, "For His divine power has bestowed on us [absolutely] everything necessary for [a dynamic spiritual] life and godliness, through true and personal knowledge of Him who called us by His own glory and excellence." AMP

Just like your butterfly sister, you have everything that you need housed in the container of our human form. You have all of the love you need. You are not missing anything. You do not need more love, more joy or more peace. You have everything you need for a dynamic spiritual life. This concept is foreign to some because you may have been taught that you need something from outside of yourself for your happiness, but that comes from a perspective of lack. You embody abundance. Everything you need is inside of you!

During the metamorphosis of *The Becoming* phase, your eyes are being reformed with new lenses that will give you the ability to see further than you have been able to see as a caterpillar. Your legs are being fashioned with the ability to run faster and cover more ground in less amount of time. Just like the butterfly gains her wings within the cocoon, you are given a new mode of transportation that will carry you higher than you have ever been before.

Newly fashioned antennae round out the additions accumulated in the cocoon. The butterfly uses her antennae to get a sense of what is going on around her during this season, you will be gifted with a new intuitive instinctiveness that will help you navigate the upcoming seasons of your life – no longer gullible. You will begin to trust yourself and the leading of the Holy Spirit in a whole new way. You will be able to stand validated, no longer needing permission from outside of yourself in order to soar.

People around you may not be able to see all of the changes that are happening in the secret place, but you will know something is happening. Just like a mighty oak tree who starts off as an acorn, you will be just like a deciduous tree who loses all signs of life during the winter season. Yet it in the dark, cold environment of winter is when what is inside the mighty oak is preparing to come forth.

If you are in the middle of your metamorphosis you may feel discombobulated, disassociated and disadvantaged but it is all part of the process. While feeling out of sorts is totally normal, this season of separation will lead to new, supportive, like-minded associations. This season of solitude and isolation is necessary to prepare you for new relationships that will be collaborative by nature.

It is best not to share with too many people about what is going on when you are in the cocoon. Those who are stuck in their caterpillar state will not have the foresight to recognize what is happening. I remember being so frustrated trying to convince other caterpillars that I was almost a butterfly. Caterpillars will try to woo you back to the safety of staying small and hidden. They will say things like, "Do not dream too big. What if it does not happen?"

However, there will be some individuals in your life that can distinguish where you currently are and where you are headed. In other words, fellow butterflies will see your butterfly, even if you are not yet fully developed. Not only will they see the essence of your butterfly but they will speak to you like the butterfly that you are.

Relationships may shift in this season. You cannot expect a caterpillar to see things from a butterfly's perspective. There is no judgment attached to a caterpillar's perspective. She will see things differently one day. But, during this phase of transition, sometimes you have to break away from the old crowd of caterpillars and make friends with some butterflies without guilt. I am not a proponent of discarding relationships, but sometimes they take on a new dynamic, and there should be no guilt in that. As your caterpillar friends see you develop your wings, you will inspire them to go through the full process of development in their cocoon, so that they too can soar one day. Just because someone has access to you in one season of your life does not guarantee them access into every season of your life.

Face to Face with All of Your "Crap" (Excuse my language, here...)

While the caterpillar is wrapped up within the borders of the cocoon, she cannot excrete. She is stuck in the cocoon with all of her feces. While this is kind of a gross thought, when you are in your season of metamorphosis and deep transformation, it is completely normal to come face to face with all of your own *crap*. When you are in the cave of the cocoon and metamorphosis is the vehicle for your becoming, you cannot seem to get rid of the parts of yourself that keep you stuck and spinning your wheels. You come face to face with all of your fears, insecurities and self-imposed limitations. The shame, guilt, and disappointment about the past rears its ugly head once again. It is a season where your self-doubt surfaces and your confidence wanes but if you will go through the full process of development and stay in the cocoon of personal transformation, something incredible will happen in the seasons to come. Instead of running from the parts of yourself that you have deemed *undesirable* and trying to eliminate the waste of your imperfections, this is an opportunity to sit with them and incorporate them into your unique individuality.

You may come in direct contact with buried anger, resentment, insecurity, fears and self-doubt. Negative emotions surface that you thought you had already dealt with. If you do not understand what is happening, you might assume that you are going backward. But you are not! You are in the right place at the right time – synchronicity is at work. Peer directly into the hollow eyes of your fears, look your anger, resentment, and bitterness dead in the face. Sit with them and feel the pain. As you stay face to face with the surge of negative emotions that surface and embrace the anguish that they bring, you will master them and you will see in the chapters to come that they will serve you. No longer will they be your master; they will benefit you in the days ahead. The word "authenticity" means to be whole. Integrating what you have been hiding from will produce a level of wholeness that will be the strength for you to soar in the days to come.

Soon it will all make sense.

Your best strategy to make it through this season is to stay put! Do not try and run from it. There is a saying that I use in coaching, "What you resist, persists!" Trust me when I tell you, you do not want to stay in the cocoon any longer than necessary! Remember what the Borg said in Star Trek, The Next Generation..." resistance is futile!" Just go with it. Even if you feel stagnate and stuck, don't worry. Change is happening. Soon you will see the results of the supernatural shifts that are taking place inside of you.

> *James 1:4 says, "But let patience have her perfect work, that ye may be perfect and entire, wanting nothing." NKJV*

Chapter 12

The Comeback

"Your setback is a set-up for your comeback." T.D. Jakes

All of the setbacks you have endured, all of your days in the solitude of the cocoon, face to face with all of your fears, insecurities, and self-doubt; all of the digging deep to discover who you are at your core has served a greater purpose. It has all been a part of the process to get you to this point right here! Transitioning through the setback so that you can come back stronger than ever is what it has all been about.

This is a unique time in the life of a butterfly and a woman who is on the rise. If you do not understand what is happening, confusion can set in and you can get sucked back into a negative cycle of frustration and discouragement.

> Romans 8:28 says, "And we know [with great confidence] that God [who is deeply concerned about us] causes all things to work together [as a plan] for good for those who love God, to those who are called according to His plan and purpose." AMP

You are in the process of becoming a fully formed butterfly. Your wings are almost complete and you have gotten almost all of the components that are necessary for functioning at a higher level. However, you are still constrained within the confines of your metamorphosis; you are still stuck in the cocoon.

The Comeback is the transitionary period between *The Becoming* and *The Debut*. This is a season of renewed hope. This is a season of redefining and redesigning. Dreams are re-awakened. *The Call* is being stirred. A woman who is preparing for her comeback has made peace with her setbacks. She is realizing that where she once saw defeat, there are actually possibilities and options available to her that she had not noticed before.

As you have been following the journey of Esther, you see that she too went through a cocoon season and experienced a metamorphosis. Her transformation was preparation for the king's presence. Let us not forget that Esther, previously named Hadassah, was an orphan girl who had suffered great loss and tragedy. Her personal transformation was more than just physical. She had to begin to see herself from a new perspective that carried with it the possibility for royalty.

Formerly orphaned, Esther may have felt abandoned or deprived by the loss of her parents. She may not have had an inheritance left to her which could have left her feeling lacking or less than the other girls that she grew up around. She was dragged away to a lonely, unfamiliar place of preparation. She was placed in a harem with many other girls her age from different parts of the kingdom. While in the harem, I can only imagine how she must have felt. Her only hope was to rescript the narrative that she had been telling herself about what had happened. She had to shift her mindset from *abandoned* to *available*. She could have felt sorry for herself or she could have seen her situation as an advantage. Esther had nothing to return to which made it easier to abandon herself and commit fully to the process of development to become a queen. Her setback had perfectly positioned her for a comeback.

Esther 2:12-15 says, "Now when it was each young woman's turn to go before King Ahasuerus, after the end of her twelve months under the regulations for the women—for the days of their beautification were completed as follows: six months with oil of myrrh and six months with [sweet] spices and perfumes and the beauty preparations for women— then the young woman would go before the king in this way: anything that she wanted was given her to take with her from the harem into the king's palace. In the evening she would go in and the next morning she would return to the second harem, to the custody of Shaashgaz, the king's eunuch who was in charge of the concubines. She would not return to the king unless he delighted in her and she was summoned by name.

Now as for Esther, the daughter of Abihail the uncle of Mordecai who had taken her in as his [own] daughter, when her turn came to go into the king, she requested nothing except what Hegai the king's eunuch [and attendant] who was in charge of the women, advised. And Esther found favor in the sight of all who saw her." AMP

Esther was whisked away into a hidden place of development. Ripped away from her family life as she knew it. She was in hiding, keeping her identity veiled to those around her lest she be mistreated because of her nationality. She was in a lonely place of preparation. For six months she was prepared with the oil of myrrh and for six months with the sweet spices and perfumes, as well as beauty preparations.[29]

This season of preparation was aided by the king's eunuch, Hegai. A eunuch was literally the bed attendant. This position was only given to one whose sexual organs had been mutilated or castrated. This was a guarantee that they were safe to care for the harem without sexually assaulting them.[30] The name "Hegai" means *separation*.[31] During your preparation for your comeback, you will be surrounded by people who are safe to be around during your season of separation. I found this to be true in my own life. As I was in preparation for my comeback, I stand in awe at the supportive people that I was surrounded with; people who did not have ulterior motives. They truly cared for me in my season of separation.

The oil of myrrh was a healing salve use to heal outward wounds. Myrrh is a resin extracted out of small, thorny tree species.[32] It's interesting to me that, once again, we see something with healing properties that originate from something that is thorny and prickly. Just like your story, He can turn our ashes into beauty. He can use the painful parts of our lives to bring healing to others.

Myrrh was also thought to be anti-inflammatory and anti-fungal.[33] It was esteemed for its purifying power. Esther was prepared for six months with an intense detoxification process. Your journey through the metamorphosis of *The Becoming* will also take you through a process of detoxification – ridding your mind of toxic thought, patterns and beliefs that keep you thinking as an orphan.

The process of beautification was a four-step process: purification, renewal, healing, and cleansing.[34] With this story taking place in the desert and sub-tropical climate, the women of the harem would have possibly had scars and wounds from intense sand-storms. These women would have been coming from all over the kingdom, so the first six months were for purification to make sure she didn't have any diseases and the second six months were for beautification. The beautification process took these women on a journey of healing from the inside out.

Your comeback is a season of preparation. Just like Esther, the process of preparing for the comeback is marked by healing from the inside out; purification, renewal, healing, and cleansing. Not one part of the process can be skipped over. Royalty demands authenticity. It is worth speculating that the previous queen, Vashti, may have jumped over a step in the process of preparation. These young women that were brought into the harem were not born into royalty. They were chosen and then prepared for the possibility of the royal title.

What are you preparing for? Restoration, recompense, and reward. If you remember, a caterpillar experiences loss when she goes into the cocoon. She loses up to half her weight when she enters into her time of development. But as she morphs into whom she was created to be, she starts adding that weight back on. She may have experienced loss, but the loss made room for more. Your setback cleared the way for the comeback that you are headed for.

In August of 2017, Houston experienced one of the worst floods that the nation had ever seen. Floods can be devastating and damaging, but I remember watching a documentary about the benefits of a flood. While they do bring destruction, they also have a way of clearing a path for new growth. I would think that a tractor and mower would suffice, but nevertheless, there are payoffs to the environment. My point is this...loss prepares the way for preparation and preparation lays the foundation for rebuilding. The caterpillar experiences loss as she goes into the cocoon. Our queenly example, Esther, suffered the loss of her family as she went into the harem. The loss experienced in your setback is what prepares you for your comeback.

Loss Doesn't Equal Failure

Many of the women that I work with have reported that the loss they have suffered in life feels like a failure. They often wince at the thought of putting themselves *out there* for fear of failure. Women often tell me that they are afraid to fail but I believe that quite the opposite is true. Women fear success. Women are afraid of their own success more than they are afraid of failure. Women are very comfortable with failing. I believe that failure feels safer than succeeding. Many times, failure feels as cozy as your favorite pair of sweatpants. It becomes an easy out; a scapegoat to which they can shift all of the blame. Women are inundated with a subconscious belief that hauntingly whispers to them, "You aren't good enough!" Self-sabotage leads to failure and failure confirms that whispered lie.

If you succeed then you have to be visible. You stand in the responsibility and authority that comes with your newly appointed position. One of my favorite business quotes is "The good news is, you are the boss, but the bad news is, you are the boss." The buck stops with the butterfly, not the cocoon. Your comeback requires a new mindset; a mindset that feels the fear of success and failure but does it anyway. You must find the treasure in your past successes and failures in order to prepare for the crown.

Your comeback is encompassed in the acceptance of your setback and the willingness to surrender to the journey between them.

Angela Aja

Phase Four

The Debut

Angela Aja

Chapter 13

The Debut

"The moment when you feel like giving up is right before your breakthrough." Victoria Arlen

The *Debut* is the fourth phase of development that a woman will walk through on her way to *The Rise*. This season of breakthrough that is marked by inauguration. This is a season of being unveiled and revealed as a more authentic version of whom you were created to be. For the woman who has entered this phase, your days of wandering and wondering are over. Just like the children of Israel, you are ready to cross over into your Promised Land. You do not have to walk in circles from this day going forward. Just like Joseph, the patriarch of old, you are now ready to be promoted from the pit to the palace. Your induction into your royal position is secure.

The word "debut" means *"a person's first appearance in a particular role or capacity."*[35] It is a grand entrance or introduction to the world. After the caterpillar has disintegrated and the cells have restructured themselves into a butterfly, she makes her grand entrance into the world as she breaks out of the cocoon and spreads her wings to fly. Once Esther was whisked away from her hometown and added to the harem of women in the king's court, she went through a process of preparation for royalty. She made her grand entrance as the newly elected queen of the kingdom. Once you have surrendered to the cocoon, endured the breakdown of the woman you were so that you could be molded into the woman you were destined to be, the next step is to make your grand entrance by showing up in the world in the most authentic way.

At this point, you have worked hard to up-level your mindset, face your fears and insecurities and go through the full process of development. Because you have learned to forgive yourself, love yourself and trust yourself in the previous phases, you are now prepared to flow in the unconventional wisdom that is available to you. You are no longer worried about pleasing other people and you can make progressive decisions even if they go against the grain. You are not looking to be understood or to be validated by the opinions of others. All of these characteristics have prepared you for your queenly anointing.

Your independent mindset from previous phases prepared you for this moment in time. You are secure in who you are, why you are here and what you are here to do so you are able to make decisions with ease. Your newly developed inter-dependent mindset has prepared you for the partnerships that you will collaborate with in *The Rise*. Now, instead of waiting on a miracle you know how to be a miracle for someone else.

The Debut is marked by practice. This is your season of rehearsing your new role as the real you, unmasked. The butterfly has never flown before. She has to practice using her wings. Esther had never been a queen. She was not born into royalty. She had to practice holding her head up high so that her crown did not fall off. You have not been accustomed to being visible and letting your voice be heard. This is your season of practicing your authenticity and being activated into a life of greater impact.

Just Shine

Your strategic action in this phase of development is simply to shine. To shine is to reveal your brilliance from within. It is that thing when people say, "You are just glowing" or "She just lights up the room."

Just like the old song I used to sing in Sunday School,

> "This little light of mine, I'm gonna let it shine. This little light of mine, I'm gonna let it shine, let it shine, let it shine, let it shine. Hide it under a bushel – NO! I'm gonna let it shine..."[36]

I used to sing that song at the top of my lungs with such determination that I would never hide my light, yet somewhere along the way, my light grew dim. I compared my light to others, diminished my light and then let others trample on my light. But once you step into *The Debut* you have a new understanding that you are responsible for keeping your own light burning bright and it is your job to protect it with valor.

Marianne Williamson said it so well.

> "Our deepest fear is not that we are inadequate. Our deepest fear is that we are powerful beyond measure. It is our light, not our darkness that most frightens us. We ask ourselves, 'Who am I to be brilliant, gorgeous, talented, fabulous?' Actually, who are you not to be? You are a child of God. Your playing small does not serve the world. There is nothing enlightened about shrinking so that other people won't feel insecure around you. We are all meant to shine, as

> children do. We were born to make manifest the glory of God that is within us. It's not just in some of us; it's in everyone. And as we let our own light shine, we unconsciously give other people permission to do the same. As we are liberated from our own fear, our presence automatically liberates others."37

Shining takes a little practice. After being small and insignificant as a caterpillar and then hiding out in the cocoon, shining does not always come naturally. That is why it is imperative not to skip over *The Debut*. You will not be as effective in *The Rise* unless you have honed your shining skills in *The Debut*. What does it mean to shine? When you awaken to your authenticity, come into alignment with your divine assignment and you are activated for the impact that you were put on this earth to make, you will reveal an inner luster. Locating this sweet spot, this intersection of your divine imprint and your divine influence reveals your divine impact – that is *The Call*.

> Matthew 5:16 says, "In the same way, let your light shine before others, that they may see your good deeds and glorify your Father in heaven." NIV

One of my clients, whom we will call "Bella," had a dilemma. She had gone through the process of discovering her mission, vision, and purpose and had identified that she was in *The Debut*. She was ready to let her light shine. She was done hiding and diminishing the gifts that God had placed inside of her to use. She had an opportunity to share her vision with a friend and confidant. This trusted comrade who had supported her all through her journey questioned Bella and discouraged her from shining so bright. She encouraged her to dim her light just a little bit so that she did not make other people uncomfortable or rock the boat. Bella's friend went as far as to shake her head in displeasure. Bella was distraught over the lack of support that she had received and considered shrinking back.

I shared with Bella Matthew 5:16 and the quote by Marianne Williamson. We talked about what options and possibilities were available to her. There was always the option of devaluing herself based on her friend's opinions of how bright she should shine, but once you have gone through the full process of development, why would you travel at the pace of a caterpillar when you have wings? Bella had to dig deep, but learning to put the oxygen mask on herself in the previous season prepared her to breathe, take a stand for her own dreams and desires in *The Debut*.

Thankfully, Bella chose to honor this new season of her life and she chose to keep shining bright. Bella has now stepped into *The Rise* and God is using her to impact women's lives like never before. She was able to practice shining in *The Debut* so that by the time she got to *The Rise*, it was as natural to her as breathing.

Another client of mine went through my twelve-week coaching program. She discovered her passion and potential. She reawakened to dreams and desires that God had placed in her since she was a young girl. She had always had a desire for fitness and a healthy lifestyle. As an average size woman, she began working out and weight-training, sculpting her body into a work of art. She got her certifications for coaching and started entering competitions. This new journey required that she put herself on display as competitive bodybuilders do. I remember many conversations about how uncomfortable she was shining. She had spent most of her life fading into the shadows, second-guessing her value and worth.

All of a sudden, she was making her grand entrance, putting herself out there for everyone to see. I am thankful that she chose to come out of obscurity and make herself visible. It has blessed me beyond measure to watch her go from inconspicuous to obvious. She made her grand entrance during her debut. She practiced shining. She is now soaring to new heights with her meticulously carved biceps and buns of steel.

You are a human being, not a human *doing*. *The Debut* is a season of just being. Whereas in previous stages, a woman gained her significance from *doing*, a woman in *The Debut* phase is learning just to be. It is not that a woman will not *do* anything in this phase. She is still actively doing life; however, any *doing* comes from who she is at her core instead of proving who she is. This is an opportunity for her to rest in the fullness of whom she was created to be, and act out of that deep authenticity as she practices showing up in the world fearlessly to make a bigger impact.

Women often tell me that they are afraid to put themselves out there. Many times, they report that they are scared to shine, to be visible and to let their voice be heard. They are worried that if they stand up to be heard, they will be judged. The fear of judgment keeps women small and hidden. Women have asked me, "How do you find the courage to let your voice be heard?" The answer is simple. When you have mined the diamonds of your past and you take ownership of your story, your purpose becomes revealed. Your purpose leads to the blossoming of your message. When you know your message, you are just a messenger. The message becomes the focus and you are able to take a backseat to the clarion call that you were created to herald from the mountaintops. It is in this season of *The Debut* that your obligation to the message outweighs your commitment to worrying about how you are perceived.

The Debut phase of development is a transitory season of preparation for *The Rise*. It is the dress rehearsal for your new role as the real you, unmasked and unfettered by fear, insecurity, and pain. *The Debut* is the bridge between who you were and whom you were meant to be. It is the practice run for your best life.

It's time to plan your coming out party, girlfriend! Get ready to celebrate!

Chapter 14

The Breakout

"What the caterpillar calls the end of the world, the Master calls a butterfly." Richard Bach

During *The Debut* phase of a woman's journey toward her rise, her expedition mimics the breaking out of the cocoon process that a newly formed butterfly goes through. This season of emerging for the butterfly is called ***eclosion***. Eclosion is when hormones are released throughout the chrysalis that cause the cocoon to become transparent so that the cocoon can begin to open.[38] As the butterfly breaks out of what once encumbered her, she now becomes unveiled to the world in full fashion. Where at one time she blended into her environment, she now displays her new colorful attire in full array. Your breaking out season reveals the beauty of whom you have become. There is no more camouflaging your gifts and talents.

I touted the title of a fashionista at one time, but while I was in my cocoon, I lost all sense of personal style. Looking back at pictures, it is as if my defeated demeanor masked the artistic, trendsetter that I had once portrayed. After breaking out of my cocoon, I had an opportunity to have a roommate for a while. She just happened to be a personal stylist from Nordstrom. She walked me through a process of discovering my unique personal style. She went through my closet as if she was cleaning out the refrigerator. She updated my look with a hair and makeup makeover. The significance of her showing up in my life at that time was huge. I believe that she came into my life to prepare me for my debut.

Your Emerging Story

Just before a butterfly is ready to start kicking her way out of the cocoon, the cocoon becomes transparent. "Eclosion is controlled by hormones. These hormones are released to soften the chrysalis and to trigger the central nervous system begin the movements needed to complete the emergence process."[39] At the time of your emerging, you will have an opportunity to become transparent about your journey, realizing that your journey – the story that once encumbered you, was the very instrument that became the container for development. This season is marked by vulnerability – an openness and defenselessness that displays itself as letting your guard down. You no longer feel the need to protect your heart or hide your journey. Your heart is now an open book to be read and enjoyed.

Whereas in previous seasons you may have felt embarrassment or shame about your story, you are now ready to embrace your story as a part of your authenticity. You realize that your story is your identity and the way you tell your story shapes your character. Your story is foundational to how you show up in the world. Science has proven that telling your story affects your physical well-being. It turns off the body's stress hormones like cortisol and epinephrine and turns on relaxation responses like oxytocin, dopamine, nitric oxide, and other endorphins. It turns on self-repair mechanisms and actually functions as preventive medicine.[40] Telling your story relaxes your nerves and heals your mind of depression, anger, and anxiety, as well as releasing feelings of connectedness.[41]

What Big Eyes You Have

The emerging butterfly has traded in her two, little beady eyes for 12,000 eyes. Yes, you read this correctly! Not just one type of eyes, two types of eyes – single and compound. One type of eye is for focus and the other type of eye is similar to the human retina with the addition of being able to see ultraviolet light.[42] Your newly formed, multi-faceted eyes allow you now see yourself through the lenses of possibility and focus on your vision. You no longer view your story through the eyes of a victim. Even if you were victimized, you are able to take responsibility for not remaining the victim. You can now embrace all of the parts of your past, the good, the bad and the ugly and bring them together in such a way that brings healing to the world.

I remember feeling such guilt and shame about my story. Growing up in the church, I did not "smoke, chew or run with those who do," as the old saying goes. Preacher's kids were known for being the worst. They had a reputation for being the rebellious ones of the bunch. But not me...I toed the line. I did not partake in the "ways of the world." I remember hearing people giving their testimony about how they were such terrible sinners and God set them on a better path. I felt so left out that I did not have a radical testimony. I guess I thought I was missing out on something.

Whew...now, looking back, I wish I would have appreciated the fact that I had a boring testimony. My world got turned upside down and out of the blue...I had a story. Once I finally had a story, I felt tremendous guilt and shame about my story. I had helped so many people keep their marriages together. How did things go so awry that I could not even save my own? I lived a "righteous" life. I prayed and fasted and did all of the things that a good Christian was supposed to do (as if those things were insurance against all hell breaking loose.)

I had become adept at telling my sad tale. I built an identity around my misery and took liberties to share with anyone who would listen. But something happened in my cocoon. During my hidden time of development, I reframed the events of my previous life. I rewrote my story from a new perspective. I penned a new version of former happenings and scripted them in such a way that I was the hero instead of the victim. I began to mine the diamonds of my past that I had once seen as lumps of coal. Once I started sharing this new version of my story, I began to witness something incredible. People found hope and courage in their own lives from hearing my story.

During *The Debut* phase of a woman's life, just like the butterfly, this is a season of being seen and heard. Owning the fullness of all of your experiences reveals the gifts that have been locked up inside of you until now. Breaking out of the cocoon of your transformation means you do not have to hide anymore. You are no longer encumbered by the container of your development. You can show up in the world and be visible without the guilt or shame of your past. Your story is now your vehicle to impact others.

It takes courage to stand in this new place of being visible and letting your voice be heard. Being hidden away, where no one can see you, might feel lonely but it also feels safe. You can protect yourself from the judgments of onlookers when you are in the cocoon. But, once you break out, being visible takes some getting used to. Showing up in the world as a more a more authentic version of yourself takes some practice. At one time you were small and insignificant but now, as a fully formed butterfly, you are more noticeable and susceptible to a new set of outside stimuli.

You Gotta Kick Your Way Out

Once the chrysalis has become transparent, there is only one way out of the cocoon. The legs come out first with forceful kicking. The butterfly pushes her way out, much like a woman pushes at the time of delivery. Just like a baby that goes through the birth canal, breaking out is no easy task, but the reward is worth the hard work. One final season of using intense exertion and force may be required in order for you to be unveiled.

After the butterfly has kicked her way out of the cocoon, she crawls all the way out exposing her abdomen and wings. Similarly, as you begin to be unveiled as the most authentic version of whom you were created to be, you may notice that you have opportunities to expose who you are at your core. Still upside down, the wings are visible but folded and wrinkled as the new butterfly begins the process of expanding her newly formed aeronautical apparatuses. Expansion begins in an upside-down process. Life may still feel topsy-turvy but it is all a part of the process. Your expansion begins while you still feel like everything is upside-down. You may have everything you need to soar to new heights, but just like the butterfly, your wings are wrinkled and clumsy. Operating in your new gifts at a high-functioning level will take some getting used to. You may have all of the components to live at a higher level but you still need the experience.

It's All A Part of the Process

The newly revealed butterfly drops to the ground from exhaustion. She takes a moment to rest and regain her strength so that she can prepare for what happens next. Once you have stepped into *The Debut* phase of life through kicking and hard work you may notice a bit of exhaustion. This is totally normal and expected after such a dedicated effort. Take time to rest and gear up for the new adventure that awaits you. Flying propels you into places you have never been before and thrusts you into a new atmosphere. Self-care is essential so that you can flow from a place of abundance and prosperity.

Through the movement of flapping the wings, they begin to dry and get unwrinkled. All of the meconium, the excretion that the butterfly was trapped with inside of the cocoon, begins to be pumped back up through the body, into the veins of the wings. The feces gets redistributed throughout the butterfly's wings and hardens.[43] Everything you have been through is what gives you the strength to fly. All of the heartache you have suffered through, all of your fears, anxieties, and insecurities...even the parts of your story that brought you so much pain gets incorporated back into the core of your being and becomes one of your greatest assets. All of the crap that you have been through now becomes incorporated into your core structure and is what supports you in flight.

While the meconium is red and looks like blood, it is merely dead cells left over from the metamorphosis.[44] The death process that you have endured; the releasing of whom you had become in order to embrace whom you were created to be, becomes the very thing that gives you the strength to soar. Whatever leftover meconium does not go back into the wings is exited out of the body of the butterfly in one swift and final thrust during its first flight. Anything that is no longer useful to you is released and you are truly free from your past.

The breaking out season is marked by risk, but staying safe no longer provides the comfort that it once did. New partnerships are formed during the season of *The Debut*. Where at one time you felt more at ease around the caterpillars, hidden in leaves and branches, now you are enjoying the freshness of the wind in your face. Not everyone from your previous seasons will celebrate your up-leveling, but it does not rock you at your core like it used to. You are not looking for the approval of others. You are not trying to get your validation from outside sources. You are getting comfortable being uncomfortable outside of your comfort zone.

Your breakthrough is here!

Chapter 15

The Crown

"A crown will not complete you or make you happy. It is simply part of the uniform of an elite group of people who are just trying to make the world a better place." Michelle Field

Training for Reigning

Not only is *The Debut* your coming-out party and your season of breaking out of the cocoon but it is also where you receive your queenly anointing and practice moving about in the palace. *The Debut* is an opportunity to get the layout of the castle– this is your training for reigning. This is where you begin to own your crown. Women have been so conditioned to think that they are not worthy of this headdress, but you cannot enter *The Rise* until you acknowledge your crown.

The Crowned Jewels

A crown is heavy-laden with jewels and you have to practice wearing it so that it is natural to walk back and forth without it falling off. Wearing the crown requires balance and good posture. This is a season of balancing who you are at your core with what you are here to do. It is a season of posturing your attitude in a way that balances humility and modesty with self-respect and self-worth.

In the season of *The Debut*, your new headdress ornately displays diamonds, rubies, emeralds, and sapphires; each one significant to this particular phase of your journey.

Diamonds

They say diamonds are a girl's best friend. There are four "C's" that are examined when choosing a diamond that reminds me of a woman on the rise.[45]

The Cut: Diamonds are cut by a master diamond cutter. Once the shape of a diamond is determined, facets (areas of the surface) are cut. It is these facets that reflect light like a prism and produces the stone's fire and brilliance. As you are fashioned into whom you were created to be, your inner light will reflect brighter and reach further.

The Color: In a diamond, less color is better because color clouds the jewel and does not allow the light to refract through it purely. While an array of colors makes our world beautiful, as it relates to a woman who is ready to shine like a diamond, clarity requires a purity of reflection. Color, in this instance, represents an opaque hallucination that clouds your judgment and hinders your vision of whom you were created to be.

The Clarity: The clarity of a diamond is measured by a "loupe," a small magnifying glass. When a flaw is detected in a diamond, it adds character to the stone and makes it unique. This helps to identify the stone. However, the flaw can affect the stone's durability. The type of flaw and the location of the flaw is more important than the flaw itself. This diamond woman understands that she must accept some flaws as a part of who she is and she can no longer walk in insecurity over these flaws. They are simply there to add character to her life and to make her unique. If she chooses to work on her flaws, it is for the purpose of being more effective, not because she doesn't think she is good enough the way she is.

The Carat Weight: The carat weight of a diamond increases the value of the stone. As you stop playing small and allow yourself to dream bigger, you bring more value to the world. The more value you bring, the more significant you feel. The more significant you feel, the more fulfilled you feel. The fulfilled you feel, the more joy you exude.

Like a diamond, a woman in *The Debut* is beginning how to appreciate the shape, size, personality, and gifts that God has given her. She has begun to allow God to mold her and cut away things that hinder her. This is evident in the way that she lives and cares unselfishly for others. Her passion for others produces a natural shine and brilliance to her life.

Rubies

A ruby represents unbridled passion and love. It symbolizes fire and blood. The ruby is said to be linked to clarity, confidence and the reclaiming of one's personal power. The price of a ruby is determined by the depth of its color. Unlike the diamond, transparency is secondary in determining the quality of this stone. Inclusions are considered to be the stone's fingerprint, rather than its flaw unless it is in the center. Defects in the stone are actually a mark of the individuality of the ruby.[46]

The Debut is marked by a woman's ability to discover her passion and tenacity. She has been through the fire and has put in the blood, sweat, and tears into life, yet is still dissatisfied. She is a woman of depth but she has suffered great loss and experienced many bumps and bruises along the way. She may have inclusions and defects from marred relationships, suffered past financial devastation or other hardships in life, but she is not about to let those things stay in the center of her being, her heart. This woman is ready to put her past behind her and see the marks in her stone as her individuality. She is ready to regain confidence and reclaim her personal power so that she can bring her unbridled passion and love to the world. She is ready to pay the price and walk in her brilliance.

Emeralds

The emerald encourages nourishing care, reflection, and growth. The emerald stone is linked to healing and balance within; specifically healing in the nervous system, digestive system, and respiratory system. It is said to help those suffering from depression, mental and emotional disorders. It is considered to be a stone of recovery, renewal, and regeneration.[47]

A woman in *The Debut* is practicing self-care, self-love, and self-respect. She has released negative mindsets about her body image and loves the skin she is in. She has a deep appreciation for herself, no longer inward, worrying about what people think about her. This gives her the ability to just be whom she was created to be without needing validation from anyone else. She no longer needs to feel anxious or worried. Her emotional state is calm and steady. She can just breathe. She is now ready to relax and set her gaze outward and upward.

Sapphires

A sapphire is a stone of wisdom, royalty and divine favor. It is associated with all things sacred and is often called the gem of gems. It is the hardest gemstone, second only to the diamond. The blue color of the sapphire signifies hope and faith. It is a symbol of power, strength, kindness and wise judgment. The blue stone is said to bring healing to the mind, mental tenacity, and focus, as well as promoting self-understanding.[48]

A woman who wears her crown is well aware that she is being summoned to soar with her newly formed wings. Just like the sapphire, she applies mental tenacity and focus. Whether it is in taking her business to the next level, healing her relationships, seeing her body restored to health, her goals are now in alignment with who she is at her core. She is well aware of her "why." Through thought-provoking conversation and deep contemplation, she clearly addresses what is going on, what is wanted and what is in the way. She is ready for a strategic action plan to bridge the gap between where she is now and where she wants to go with wisdom, royalty and divine favor.

According to Town and Country magazine, any woman can wear a tiara or a crown but "ancient tradition has it that they must be a bride or already married. The tiara has its roots in classical antiquity and was seen as an emblem of the loss of innocence to the crowning of love."[49] When you step into "The Debut" phase of your life, your crown becomes a declaration of your new supremacy over your thoughts, patterns, and beliefs that once kept you small and insignificant. You are no longer innocently led unaware into the emotional traps that once ensnared you.

The Crown Gives You Access to Places You Have Never Been

Not only does training for reigning take practice, but it also involves risk. You have to get comfortable in the uncomfortable. You have to risk venturing to places you have never gone before. Coming from the cocoon, tight places with limited mobility may be restrictive but they also become comfortable. The crown gives you access to roam the halls of a more expansive dwelling – the castle. Living in a more spacious place with freedom of movement invites you to exploration and curiosity. This season provides an opportunity to move about with a sense of flow.

Studies have proven that people who previously had very little money and suddenly win the lottery or gain some other form of immediate wealth, rapidly lose it by squandering it. I believe this is because they did not take the time to go through the full process of development and transformation. It gives credence to the importance of enduring *The Cave, The Becoming* and *The Debut* as preparation for *The Rise*.

Let us pick back up with our story of Esther. After going through the full process of preparation and transformation, she was ready for her debut in front of the king.

> *Esther 2: 17 "Now the king loved Esther more than all the other women, and she found favor and kindness with him more than all the [other] virgins, so that he set the royal crown on her head and made her queen in the place of Vashti. 18 Then the king held a great banquet, Esther's banquet, for all his officials and his servants; and he made a festival for the provinces and gave gifts in accordance with the resources of the king." NIV*

Esther had been chosen as the new queen, her head dressed ornately with the crown. Up until this time, Esther had hidden her true identity as a Jew. Just as the cocoon becomes transparent right before the butterfly breaks out of the cocoon and reveals her wings to the world, Queen Esther was about to be given an opportunity to come out of hiding, divulge her true identity and use her voice to save her people from utterly being destroyed. Once you have gone through the full process of development and you have discovered who you are, why you are here and what you are here to do, there will be an opportunity for you to be vulnerable. Transparency is an opportunity to take off the masks that have hidden your authenticity. It is your moment to show up in the world in true freedom.

The villain in Esther's story is a power-hungry man named Haman. Haman had convinced the king to sign a proclamation for all Jews to be annihilated. Queen Esther's uncle, Mordecai, learned of Haman's plot to have the Jews killed. He sent word to Queen Esther through her attendants about evil Haman's plans. Since the king was not aware of her Jewish heritage, the proclamation was a kiss of death for the queen as well as her entire people group. When you hide your true identity, the impact far outweighs your own life. It is imperative, even a matter of life or death, once you have developed into your truest identity to disclose who you are to the world.

Queen Esther discussed the matter with her maids and eunuchs and sent word back to Mordecai.

> *Esther 4:12-14 "When Esther's words were reported to Mordecai, 13 he sent back this answer: 'Do not think that because you are in the king's house you alone of all the Jews will escape. 14 For if you remain silent at this time, relief and deliverance for the Jews will arise from another place, but you and your father's family will perish.* ***And who knows but that you have come to your royal position for such a time as this?'****NIV [emphasis added]*

4:15 Then Esther sent this reply to Mordecai: 16 "Go, gather together all the Jews who are in Susa, and fast for me. Do not eat or drink for three days, night or day. I and my attendants will fast as you do. When this is done, I will go to the king, even though it is against the law. And if I perish, I perish."

17 So Mordecai went away and carried out all of Esther's instructions." NIV

It was customary for Esther to wait to be called upon by the king. To approach him unannounced could cost her life. But that did not stop her. She did not wait and she did not hesitate. During the season of "The Debut," the crown demands action, but not just any action – strategic action. Instead of running and blurting out her demands, Queen Esther took deliberate action. She went to the king. When the king saw her, he was pleased and extended his golden scepter to her. Esther requested the king's presence, along with Haman, at a banquet. The king offered her up to half his kingdom but instead, she tactically invited them back the next day for another banquet. Her timing was impeccable.

Meantime, Haman saw Mordecai on the way home from the banquet. Remembering how much he hated Mordecai, he had gallows built to hang him.

When the King Can't Sleep

Consider the faithfulness of Mordecai, Queen Esther's uncle who was instrumental in her rise. This story reminds me that the seeds that we sow will grow up and reap a harvest even if we do not see the fruit of our labor right away. Prior to Esther's rise into the kingdom, Mordecai had been responsible for stopping a plot to assassinate the king, but he had never been rewarded for his good deeds. One night the king could not sleep and he asked for the book of the annals – just some simple nighttime reading. He just happened to open the book to the story of Mordecai's intervention of the scoundrels who plotted to kill the king. Divine synchronicity was at work.

> Esther 6: 3 "What honor and recognition has Mordecai received for this?" the king asked.
> "Nothing has been done for him," his attendants answered.
> 4 The king said, "Who is in the court?" Now Haman had just entered the outer court of the palace to speak to the king about impaling Mordecai on the pole he had set up for him.
> 5 His attendants answered, "Haman is standing in the court."
> "Bring him in," the king ordered.
> 6 When Haman entered, the king asked him, "What should be done for the man the king delights to honor?"
> Now Haman thought to himself, "Who is there that the king would rather honor than me?" 7 So he answered the king, "For the man the king delights to honor, 8 have them bring a royal robe the king has worn and a horse the king has ridden, one with a royal crest placed on its head. 9 Then let the robe and horse be entrusted to one of the king's most noble princes. Let them robe the man the king delights to honor, and lead him on the horse through the city streets, proclaiming before him, 'This is what is done for the man the king delights to honor!'"

10 "Go at once," the king commanded Haman. "Get the robe and the horse and do just as you have suggested for Mordecai the Jew, who sits at the king's gate. Do not neglect anything you have recommended." NIV

Haman, thinking that the king wanted to honor him, painted a picture of royal display for the king. He was now forced to honor the man that he had set out to destroy. Talk about recompense and reward...I can just picture the dismay on Haman's face when he was commanded to honor the man whom he had loathed and plotted to kill.

Haman's Evil Plot is Discovered

The king and Haman attended yet another banquet provided by the queen. The king was so impressed that he offered her anything she wanted, even up to half of the kingdom.

3 Then Queen Esther answered, "If I have found favor with you, Your Majesty, and if it pleases you, grant me my life—this is my petition. And spare my people—this is my request. 4 For I and my people have been sold to be destroyed, killed and annihilated. If we had merely been sold as male and female slaves, I would have kept quiet, because no such distress would justify disturbing the king.[a]"
5 King Xerxes asked Queen Esther, "Who is he? Where is he—the man who has dared to do such a thing?"
6 Esther said, "An adversary and enemy! This vile Haman!"
Then Haman was terrified before the king and queen. 7 The king got up in a rage, left his wine and went out into the palace

> garden. But Haman, realizing that the king had already decided his fate, stayed behind to beg Queen Esther for his life.
>
> 8 Just as the king returned from the palace garden to the banquet hall, Haman was falling on the couch where Esther was reclining. The king exclaimed, "Will he even molest the queen while she is with me in the house?"

The king was outraged and ordered Haman to be impaled; he was impaled on the very gallows that he had built for Mordecai. As a woman on her journey toward *The Rise*, trust that as you bravely walk in your newly appointed position, whatever comes against you will not succeed.

Like Esther, you have come into the kingdom for such a time as this. You have a purpose to fulfill. The season of *The Debut* and the accepting of your crown aligns you with your calling. No matter what problems arise, strategic action and divine synchronicity become your *modus operandi*. You are learning to think and act like a queen.

Angela Aja

Phase Five

The Rise

Angela Aja

Chapter 16

The Rise

"There is no force equal to a woman determined to rise." W.E.B. Dubois

There are distinct indicators of entering the phase of *The Rise*. This final phase is marked by a season of greater impact. This is the time when a woman steps into the fullness of whom she was created to be. She is led by a sense of mission, vision, and purpose. She is motivated intrinsically to step into *The Call* that has been evolving within her during the previous phases of development. This is a season of advancement, acceleration, and abundance. Her perception is from the perspective of oversight. She is no longer training for reigning but governing her life and her business with self-leadership and administrating her life with poise and divine direction.

To bring things full circle, if you remember from the introduction of the book, a woman who has completed this journey now possesses the following qualities. She is now:

Resilient – A woman on the rise is resilient about her past. If you are resilient you have come through some stuff; you have experienced life. Deep down inside, a resilient woman knows that her setbacks prepared her for her comeback. If you are resilient, you know who you are – you are strong, you have tenacity; you have natural buoyancy that gives you the ability to snap back. Something in your gut tells you that where you are in your journey is not your final destination. You are compelled to overcome obstacles and breakthrough barriers which try to limit you to a life of ordinary.

Intentional – A woman on the rise is intentional about her future. I have heard people say things like, "Well, if it is God's will…" Happenstance and haphazardness should not be indicators of God's will in your life. You are intentional, deliberate, focused and committed to the full process of development in order to step into your call. It is possible for you to know with assurance who you are at your core, why you are here and what you are here to do.

A tug of war between your destiny and your day to day grind will always entice you to succumb to the disruption of the pointless obligations – but you are a woman on the rise – intentional about your focus and the direction you move in.

Spirit-led – A woman on the rise is Spirit-led in her endeavors. If you are a Spirit-led woman you do not lean on your own understanding in your decision-making process. You are Kingdom-minded with eternal values and priorities. You are perceptive, guided by your intuition and you have learned to trust yourself. You are not daunted by what you see, you exhibit faith in the unseen. As a Spirit-led woman, you do not always follow conventional wisdom. You are not influenced by the approval or the dissatisfaction of others. A woman on the rise is a Spirit-led woman who is committed to a vision that encompasses a vastness that extends far beyond her own individual life.

Empowered – A woman on the rise is empowered to show up in the world fearlessly and make a bigger impact. As a woman on the rise, you know that you are empowered for the job. You are not afraid of your personal power. You have a revelation that the acknowledgment of your personal power does not detract from the power of God; rather it is an outward expression of the power of God that resides inside of you. As an empowered woman, you use your power to influence your own past, present, and future. You influence your own thoughts, patterns, and behaviors so that the influence you have over your own life begins to exude out of you and impact those within your sphere of influence. As a woman on the rise, you are empowered from within.

Identifiers of *The Rise*

Advancement

The Rise brings advancement and promotion. There is no apology needed for stepping into significance, fulfillment and true joy. The elevation of this season is not for self-indulgent praise, but for the propagation of purpose and impact. This new perspective allows you to see things from a new vantage point so that you can use your position to create change and cause dynamic atmospheric shifts.

Acceleration

Just as the queen in the game of chess has maneuverability, this season brings an acceleration of movement and freedom of accessibility into areas that were previously not available to you. Things seem to happen at quantum levels. Doors begin to open that you did not even know were options for you. There is a sense of perfect timing and divine synchronicity that produces miracles.

Amos 9:13-15 says, "Yes indeed, it won't be long now," God's decree. "Things are going to happen so fast your head will swim one thing fast on the heels of the other. You won't be able to keep up. Everything will be happening at once—and everywhere you look there are blessings! Blessings like wine pouring off the mountains and hills. I'll make everything right again for my people Israel." MSG

Achievement

This is where inspiration turns to implementation and achievement is birthed. Tragedy has turned to triumph. There is a sense of attainment and accomplishment that creates a foundation for the real work to begin. Most of the work, up until now, has been an internal venture. However, this season becomes a time of living from the inside-out. You know how to give from a place of abundance and live from a place of overflow; this produces dynamic results.

Visibility

Visibility becomes a natural by-product of stepping into *The Rise*. When you step into *The Rise*, significance comes from your impact, not your visibility. As I saw acceleration and achievement begin to unfold in my own life, there came a point where I was beginning to get some notoriety. I was being invited on talk shows, radio shows, Facebook Live interviews; I was frequently invited to step into more visible places. Some friends asked me if I was "on top of the moon" about all that was happening. While I was excited about all of the opportunities that were opening up to me, I realized that being in the spotlight did not make me feel more significant or more valuable. I knew that the visibility was a result of my significance, value and worth rather than the *proof* of my significance, value, and worth. The journey you take to get to the phase of *The Rise* brings you through a process of gaining a deep understanding and appreciation of yourself in the cocoon and you practice standing in it during *The Debut*, by the time you step into *The Rise*, visibility becomes a by-product of flowing in *The Call*. You do not need validation from the crowds because you are validated intrinsically. Standing in the limelight is not about performance. You are playing an authentic role that requires no masks to hide behind.

Glory in the Story

Where once there had been shame and guilt in regards to my story, there were now precious gems. I had gone through the process of mining the diamonds of my past which I had previously seen as ugly lumps of coal. I had re-scripted the events of my journey in a way that would bring God all the glory of my story. I had written down excerpts of my life from time to time, but I had no formal structure to my writings. I knew there was a book inside of me that was waiting to be written, but I had no idea how to put my guts on paper in a way that would inspire and motivate a reader. However, something miraculous was about to happen.

It was the Saturday before Easter. I remember waking up and going to my computer. A divine download began pouring out of my heart and my fingers flew across the keyboard. *Summoned to Soar: The Five Stages of the Rise of a Woman* was born. All of a sudden, my whole life made sense. That day, the words came gushing out of me like a flowing river. Every story, every event of my life and every lesson that I had learned, fit into these five phases of development. But there was one phase that I did not have any stories for – *The*

Rise. The next morning was Easter Sunday morning. I heard the voice of God in a still, small voice that said, "Not only does today mark the remembrance of My resurrection, but today also marks the beginning of your resurrection and restoration. Today is the first day of *The Rise*." I knew at that moment that I had stepped into a new season. Now it was up to God to provide me with stories for this new phase of development.

When I stepped into *The Rise*, nothing happened immediately. I was living with my parents and things did not seem to be changing much, but somehow, just knowing that I had stepped into a new phase of development brought a new awareness to who I was and what I was called to do. Clarity flooded my soul.

Now that I had the framework for my story, the keys on my computer became like the keys of a piano and I began to compose the instrumental of my life. There was still something missing. What was I going to do with all of these words? I had the scaffolding of my story erected and construction on the telling of it had begun, but what would happen next? Was I writing all of this to take up gigabytes on my computer?

Collaboration

Collaboration is significant in the stage of *The Rise*. Collaboration is a partnership. Partnerships thrive when you step into interdependence. Whereas in the previous stages you operated from a mindset of co-dependence, dependence or independence, interdependence now connects you to associations and affiliations that flow in mutual areas of impact.

One of my clients, a dear friend, had been through my coaching programs. As a result of doing the work, she recouped her initial investment thirty times and her ordinary life was exploding into a life of extraordinary. She texted me one day and asked if she could set a phone meeting with me in regards to my book, which she had heard me mention that I was writing. The day arrived for our phone conversation. The words that she spoke next had my mouth hanging wide open.

She said to me, "I would like to **COLLABORATE** with you on your book." My response was, "Ummmmm.... YES! YES! YES!" As a result of the coaching program, she had discovered her skill set of knowing how to publish books was not limited to just the cold realm of authority marketing but could be paired with her divine calling of helping people share their stories in order to inspire a Kingdom mindset. She wanted to start her business but she needed someone to take through the process of self-publishing, from start to finish as preparation for her own program. She had the publishing skills and I had a book that needed to be published! Our collaboration became a partnership that formed a foundation for both of us to show up in the world fearlessly to make a bigger impact.

There was no way that I could have made this happen on my own. Our collaboration began. She gave me tools, timelines and tricks of the trade to fill in the missing pieces of the unfolding of my story. She was "the ying to my yang." Together, we were able to put all of our random pieces of the puzzle together and create a dynamic representation of how our individual purposes would come together in a beautiful portrait of influence and impact.

Restoration

The Rise is a unique phase to step into. It is a culmination of all of the previous phases coming together. *The Rise* is a season of restoration, where the fullness of time meets the fullness of preparation. *The Rise* is marked by abundance, visibility, divine connections, legacy building and the enjoyment of life – the fruits of your labor.

As I sat smack dab in the middle of my *rise*, my surroundings were not in alignment with my new phase of development. Quite the contrary; I was living in a bedroom in my parent's house, barely making ends meet. Momentum was building. People's lives were being impacted on a daily basis, but my situation seemed to stay the same.

I knew in my gut that it was my time to rise. I knew that just as it was spoken of Queen Esther, that I had come into the Kingdom for such a time as this. Everyone I talked to seemed to see an aura of enlargement and intensification. I began to have strange occurrences where people would look at me and say the same thing. They would say, "You have no idea what is about to happen to you. God has surprise, after surprise, after surprise for you. It is not *going* to happen, it is happening now."

I was keenly aware that in order for me to rise, I needed to be in my own place. When a butterfly takes flight her location changes from hanging upside down on a branch to soaring to new heights. I knew that it was time for me to move.

I woke up one Friday morning and a Spirit of Faith overwhelmed me. I prayed, "Father, in the next seven days, I want to know where I am moving to. I want to know where the place of my rise will be." The next morning, I walked out of the front door and there was a flyer for a moving company lying on the front porch. I knew it was a sign. As a step of faith, I started looking online at houses to rent. There was one house that kept showing up and the only way to explain it is that there was a light shining on this house. It looked like the perfect place for me. I called a friend who was a real estate agent; a single mom whom I knew would be blessed by the commission. I asked her if she would schedule an appointment to see the house. She called me a few days later and said there was a problem with her license and that I would need to call the owner directly.

Now, there were some obvious roadblocks to my renting my own place. First of all, my credit was less than perfect due to the drama that had erupted after my divorce. Second of all, I did not have any rental history for the last nine months because I had been living in my parent's house. I looked terrible on paper.

The following Friday, the seventh day, something drew me back to that house. I decided to look up the owner's information and call them directly to schedule an appointment to see the house. My eyes could hardly believe what they were beholding. The owners of the home were my very dear friends. I called and scheduled a tour of the home. When I walked in, I knew that this was the place of my *rise*. I felt it with every fiber of my being. But it would take a miracle.

As she and I stood in the house, I was completely honest with her about my situation. This was a step of faith on my behalf and I was looking for someone to collaborate with me by not considering my financial history. If it was left up to her, she would have said yes in an instant, but this property was their retirement plan and her husband did not budge when it came to the perfect renters. He considered it a "must" to have a renter with excellent credit. With three other worthy offers for the house on the table, my dear friend was almost sure that her husband would not consider me for the house. We prayed together before we left, believing that if this house was to be mine then God would have to make it happen.

Even though I knew that this was my new dwelling place and I was certain that it would take a miracle. I completely released it and let go of any attachment to the outcome. About an hour later, my dear friend texted me and said the house was mine to rent. She had talked to her husband and she did not even have to twist his arm. He walked away from three other impeccable offers to rent the house and immediately took the house off the market. Not only that, but the greatest miracle was that he did not even care to take my financial history into consideration.

Just like the remains of the caterpillar are nowhere to be found upon the butterfly's being, my past was no longer being considered as a determining factor to my future. When you step into *The Rise*, your past is the past. My past was no longer lingering, keeping me restricted or restrained. I was free to move about without limitation.

The All-inclusive Cruise

My dad used to tell a story about a man who bought a ticket to go on his first cruise. It had been a lifelong dream to see the world. As he boarded the vessel, he marveled at the richness and elegance that surrounded him. He unloaded all of his bags and belongings in his room. He had brought an array of fruit and snacks to sustain him on his journey. He would walk past the tables lined with delicacies and see everyone rushing to the dinner line. He marveled at the exquisite array of beautifully styled food as his stomach growled. But he did not let himself care. He was on the ship and seeing the world. That was all that mattered.

As the days went on, he began to run out of food. He would go back to his room and eat an apple, wait until dinner was over and then go back out to mix and mingle and view the sunset before retiring to his room for the night. Soon the rations he brought were completely depleted. The man eventually died of starvation on that cruise.

The man never dared to dream that his ticket included his meals. The entire trip he had permission and access to all the choice foods laid out before him, but night after night he contented himself with the meager provisions he brought aboard. He had stepped into his dream but failed to partake of all of the benefits that accompanied it. *The Rise* comes with all-inclusive benefits. You have already paid the price of going through the full process of development. This is a season of enjoying the fruits of your labor. *The Rise* is a season of advancement, achievement, and acceleration. It is a time of visibility and collaboration that brings a flow of abundance. This is your time. This is your season.

Chapter 17

The Wings and the Wind

"A caterpillar does all the work but the butterfly gets all the publicity." George Carlin

As discussed in the previous chapter, the fifth phase of the rise of a woman is *The Rise*. This is the season where you are summoned to soar. It is a season of collaboration between the wings of the butterfly and the wind. While a butterfly can rise to new heights with her new instruments of flight, in order for the winged creature to operate at her full capacity, she needs to partner with the wind. Cooperating with the tailwinds can increase her speed up to sixty miles per hour which allows her to conserve her energy.[50]

As you enter *The Rise* phase of your development, you may be able to go higher than you have ever gone before but when you partner with the wind of the Spirit, God will quicken your destiny and make time stand still so that you can fulfill the purpose that you were divinely created for. In the Bible, the book of Joshua, Chapter 10, tells a story of how God made time stand still so that Joshua could finish the battle and prevail over his enemies. Whatever came against you in previous phases will not prevail over you in *The Rise* and you do not have to fight your battles alone. As you collaborate with Heaven, a divine acceleration will make up for lost time.

As mentioned in the previous chapter, not only did I receive the Divine download about the pages of this book, but I partnered with the wind – the wind of the Spirit which connected me to collaborating partnerships to bring the dream of this book into a reality. Zechariah 4:6 took on a whole new meaning.

It says,

> "'Not by might nor by power, but by My Spirit,' says the LORD of hosts." KJV

This is the time when everything you have gone through has prepared you for this moment. Where you had to learn how to surrender to the full process in the first phase, now you have to surrender to the wind. The wind moves at its own pace. It beats to its own drum. The wind cannot be seen with physical eyes but you know where it is by the movement that is created. The wind cannot be summoned but the wind summons you to a new elevation.

As you are being summoned to soar, you are called to a higher level. This ascension brings about leadership opportunities. Leadership that has its roots in the self-leadership developed within the previous stages, produces an empathetic humility, resulting in true servant-leadership. To soar is to be elevated but elevated is not better, it is just different.

I love how my friend, Rick Renner, describes the role of a minister or a leader.

> "Let a man so account of us, as of the ministers of Christ, and stewards of the mysteries of God. — *1 Corinthians 4:1*

When I was first starting to study New Testament Greek many years ago, I pulled out my Greek New Testament one day and flipped it over to First Corinthians 4:1. There I discovered that the Greek word for "ministers" was the word huperetas — the Greek word that was used to depict the very lowest class of criminals. I knew Paul must have had a reason for selecting this word to describe "ministers," but it made me wonder.

Similarly, if you are going to move ahead with what God has called you to do — whether it is your ministry, your family, or your business — you must learn how to be a faithful servant, working together with others as a team "in the bottom of the boat."[51]

The Rise is not about glory and fame. The leadership that comes in *The Rise* often feels more like the role of an under-oarsman in the bottom of the boat. You lead from a position of support. *The Rise* is an opportunity to use your visibility to make a bigger impact. It is about using your wings to inspire neighboring caterpillars to continue on their journey and to encourage them to surrender to the full process of development so they, too, can shed their cocoon and soar to new heights by your side.

Postured, Poised and Perpendicular

Taking flight requires good posture and a little bit of waggle from the butterfly. Waggle is when the butterfly positions herself perpendicular to the ground, twisting her flapping wings to create miniature whirlwinds that will lift her off of the ground. The butterfly goes from upside down to straight up and down. This new vertical alignment enables the butterfly to go higher than she has ever gone before.[52]

In preparation for rising higher than you have ever been as a woman, it is imperative to be properly positioned – poised and perpendicular to the ground. Even if standing erect feels out of your comfort zone, this is an upright season of life that suits your new queenly anointing. Positioning reveals your authority. Being perfectly positioned at the right place and at the right time happens instinctively now as you are directed by divine guidance.

> *Galatians 5:25 says, "If we live by the Spirit, let us also keep in step with the Spirit." ESV*

The word "positioned" means "an act of placing or arranging". It is "the point or area that is occupied."[53] As you prepare for a flight into a realm that you have only been to in your dreams, it is imperative to occupy or own this new way of being. This is your new home; your new habitation. You will now take up residence at a higher level. As you are summoned to soar, catching the tailwind of the Spirit requires trust and surrender; trusting that the wind – that which is unseen – can carry you now. There is a new activation of faith, leaving behind what feels concrete and solid for that which is invisible to the naked eye.

Butterflies Bask

Butterflies bask in the sun. They rely on the heat absorbed from the sun to keep them warm.[54] They sit in the sun with outstretched wings, soaking it in to raise their internal temperature. As a woman in *The Rise*, you bask in the warmth of God's presence. You rely on the source of the Spirit of God to fuel you from the inside-out. You are well aware that the strength you now have goes beyond your natural capabilities. Soaring at this level is not something you can do in your own strength. This is a season of deep intercession and worship that provides you with a supernatural grace for the mission set before you. With arms outstretched, basking requires no effort on your part. It is a time of stillness and rest as you soak in the warmth of God's love.

Psalms 46:10 says, "Be still and know that I am God." KJV

The Butterfly Effect

These dancing queens of the animal world do not fly in a straight line. Butterflies do not flap their wings up and down like birds. They make their bodies stiff and make figure-eight patterns with their wings; making them swim through the air. Their erratic flight patterns keep them safe from would-be predators. They constantly adjust their center of gravity by shifting the position of their wings which gives them the ability to turn on a dime and create turbulence. In other words, they can stir up the atmosphere. The Butterfly Effect is real. The wind created from a single motion of the wings of a butterfly can have a huge impact on the weather in other parts of the world.[55]

In *The Rise* season, your partnership with the wind of the Spirit will bring a new flow. It will create an apostolic anointing to stir things up, shifting the atmosphere to create spiritual movement and momentum all over the world. What might seem to be erratic flight patterns to some, as a woman on the rise, you can no longer make decisions based on the approval of others. Being Spirit-led is the only way that you will stay out in front of the traps of the enemy. Making decisions that are not based on unconventional wisdom will cause dynamic supernatural shifts that could not happen in ordinary circumstances. Just as the butterfly swims through the air making a figure-eight pattern with her wings, the number eight is the number of resurrections. Your movements will now cause a resurgence of renewal and restoration.

Where at one time you may have felt as though you were fighting an uphill battle, there is an effortless flow to life. Aligned with authenticity, you are no longer stuck and spinning your wheels. You have the freedom of movement, even if it does not make sense to the outside world. You know how to shift through transitions with grace and ease. You are not afraid to stir things up. Your commitment to living a life of purpose far outweighs your fear of rocking the boat. You are fully aware that creating holy turbulence is all a part of your new job description. You are committed to stirring up the atmosphere so that your impact far extends your reach.

Abundance

A butterfly does not need the entirety of her wingspan. If half of her wing was removed, she could still fly without a problem. Now abundantly adorned with her colorful extensions of aeronautical design, her wings are disproportionately excessive in relation to her body.[56] Flying to new heights, the beautiful butterfly that was once hidden now has extreme visibility.

Just as the newly revealed butterfly has an abundance of wings, *The Rise* phase is demonstrated with increase and abundance. Abundance is not something you are trying to get, but rather something that comes from within. It is your natural state. Where lack and deficiency were once keeping you hidden and small, *The Rise* is a season of generating and circulating finances, creating financial momentum and global impact. This new visibility brings a distinguishable and conspicuous anointing that is often the prelude to prominence. The prominence does not come from fame or celebrity status, but rather for the purpose of impact and societal change.

Whereas the main job of the caterpillar was to eat and grow, the foremost purpose of the butterfly is to drink sweet nectar, find her mate and lay eggs. The purpose of a woman who has entered *The Rise* phase of her life is now the enjoyment of life, to connect with divine partnerships, and leave a legacy. Where struggle and turmoil were once her food, she can now dine at the banqueting table of the fruit of her labor from a new perspective as she partners with the wind and soars to new heights. Connecting with other butterflies is the name of the game now. Finding your tribe, your "soaring mates," that are linked to your purpose is part of the process now. Depositing the seeds of wisdom that you have learned along the way will leave an inheritance that far outlives you.

This is your season to soar. Enjoy your flight!

Chapter 18

The Collaboration

"If I have seen further, it is by standing on the shoulders of giants." – Isaac Newton

Collaboration is the act of partnering with a person or a team on a project.[57] Collaboration happens when alliances are made and people come together for a common goal. Collaborating takes place in an atmosphere of interdependence and teamwork. Everything you have gone through on your journey to *The Rise* has prepared you for collaboration. Collaboration supports you as you operate from *The Call* to show up in the world fearlessly and make a bigger impact.

Queen Esther

Just as you read in the previous chapter, *The Rise* is a season marked by collaboration. You read about the collaboration between the butterfly and the wind, taking her to new heights. Bringing the story of Queen Esther to a close, it is evident that she too, accessed the power of collaboration as she stood in her royal position. Her collaboration with the king resulted in the endowment of a new authority that gave her the ability to save an entire nation from annihilation.

> Esther 8 says,"
> *3Esther again pleaded with the king, falling at his feet and weeping. She begged him to put an end to the evil plan of Haman the Agagite, which he had devised against the Jews. 4Then the king extended the gold scepter to Esther and she arose and stood before him.*
> *5"If it pleases the king," she said, "and if he regards me with favor and thinks it the right thing to do, and if he is pleased with me, let an order be written overruling the dispatches that Haman son of Hammedatha, the Agagite, devised and wrote to destroy the Jews in all the king's provinces. 6For how can I bear to see disaster fall on my people? How can I bear to see the destruction of my family?"*
> *7King Xerxes replied to Queen Esther and to Mordecai the Jew, "Because Haman attacked the Jews, I have given his estate to Esther, and they have impaled him on the pole he set up. 8Now write another decree in the king's name in behalf of the Jews as seems best to you, and seal it with the king's signet ring—for no document written in the king's name and sealed with his ring can be revoked."*

When Queen Esther found out that the annihilation of the Jews was in full swing, she fell on her face weeping before the king. For just a moment, she stepped back into an emotional outburst that had its roots in fear. It is not uncommon, as you transition from *The Debut* into *The Rise*, still practicing your queenly graces, to "have a moment." *You know, girls...we have all had "our moments."* God blessed the female race with the ability to be deeply connected to your emotions, but your emotions are NOT your identity.

You HAVE emotions. You DO emotions, but you are not your emotions. How many times have you labeled yourself by your emotions and made them your identity? "I AM angry!" "I AM sad." "I AM fearful." "I AM frustrated." As a queen, you have the ability to rule over your emotions. You are not there to serve your emotions. You have emotions to help you navigate through life, to bless you and enjoy the human experience.

Ok...back to the story...

The gracious king extended his golden scepter and told her to get up. After her little episode, Queen Esther stood up and brushed herself off. Once she was standing erect, as a queen should be, she asked for what she wanted with boldness.

Declaration

Whereas in previous seasons you were practicing keeping your word, particularly to yourself, it was all in preparation for this moment in time. Your subconscious mind hears what you say and knows that you will follow through. You keep your word and do what you say. Now, you can do what the Bible says,

> Job 22:28, "You will also decide and decree a thing, and it will be established for you; And the light [of God's favor] will shine upon your ways. AMP

Declaration becomes your new language of leadership. A declaration is a pronouncement. It is an assertion that commands action. It is a notification of a request that is to be granted. When you declare something, you speak it into existence. All of the preparation through self-leadership in the previous stages, established a foundation for true influence over yourself and your word so that impact could exude out of you.

Not only did the king grant Queen Esther's wish but he gave her complete control over what the details would look like. He told her to go write the decree the way she wanted it to look. In this season, you get the *say-so*. You have the ability to design it and define in a way that aligns with your mission, vision, and purpose. She wrote the new pronouncement for the salvation of her people and then she was given access to the king's signet ring to seal the deal. She wrote the decree and the king approved it.

Authority

Queen Esther now stood fully initiated in her royal position. The king granted her the authority to reverse the curse that had been set up against her people. The king gave Queen Esther his signet ring to seal whatever deal she had written. She was handed an authority that far outweighed her own dominion.

Every part of your journey – every phase that you go through prepares you for *The Rise*. When you step into *The Rise* all of the lessons that you learned in *The Ordinary* come back to you. You remember lessons from *The Cave* about how to acquiesce and surrender to the WHOLE process. You have learned how to stop all of the wiggling and the squirming and you "let go and let God" during *The Becoming*. During *The Debut* phase, you practice how to ask for what you want without shame or guilt. You now recognize that you deserve to ask for what you want. In the season of *The Rise*, you will be granted the ability to ask and given the royal seal of approval.

Your words now carry the weight of authority. This is a time to choose your words carefully. There is an accountability that comes with this new authority. Another word for "accountability" is "liability."[58] I was so confused when I first read that, but then it made sense. Liability is an obligation or a debt. It is a price that is worth paying. There is a weightiness of responsibility that your words carry that will pump people up or pull them down. Queen Esther stood in her new-found authority and made a declaration. She made a pronouncement of life that saved a nation from destruction. You too have the same opportunity. This is your moment of purpose. This is the time to heal the wounds you are here to reconcile, to answer the questions you have got the solutions to, and to tell the story that you are here to share and to herald the message you are here to proclaim. This is where your ashes turn to beauty.

> Esther 4:14b, "And who knows but that you have come to your royal position for such a time as this?" NIV

Queen, you have stepped into the right place at the right time. Your hard work was not in vain. Your hard work is about to pay off.

Expansion

After the drama ensued and Haman's evil plot was exposed and reversed, not only was Queen Esther given access to the king's domain, but she was granted the estate of her enemy. Where you were once limited to one location, now with your queenly anointing, you can come and go as the wind summons. The kingdom is your new domain. The castle is the headquarters – your base of operations. You have been given the keys of the kingdom to do the King's bidding, expanding His territory as you go. Your collaboration, in the final phase of *The Rise*, lays a foundation for you to live out the rest of your days with authenticity, purpose, and intention.

As a woman in *The Rise*, it is time to get up! This is not a time to beg and plead with God to answer your prayers. Your days of groveling are over. Groveling just gets your gown dirty. A queen curtsies and genuflects in the presence of the king – she does not roll around on the ground. Stand upright with your crown steadied and secure so that you rise up and stand in your relegated authority to ask for what you want with clarity and confidence. The keys of the Kingdom have been given to you. As you collaborate with the King, abundance, expansion, and authority accompany the royal scepter that you now possess. You have changed the outcome of your legacy. You are a woman living in *The Rise*.

Conclusion

Angela Aja

Chapter 19

Summoned to Soar

"One cannot consent to creep when one feels an impulse to soar." Helen Keller

As you enter the final stage, *The Rise* is not a destination, but a culmination. It is the zenith from where you live your most impactful life. It is a phase of phases within the journey of life.

The Difference between a Moth and a Butterfly

As I close, I want to leave you with one final thought. As I studied the evolution of the butterfly, I discovered that the moth goes through the same metamorphosis process. There are, however, some important differences between the moth and the butterfly. While the transformation process is the same, the main purpose of a moth is to be a super-food for other insects and animals. As women who are on *The Rise*, it is your time to nourish yourself so that you can nourish others. Gone are the days that you are a super-food to everyone else, giving and giving while neglecting yourself.

Moths are only nocturnal [59] – they do not bask in the sun like a butterfly does. They are more comfortable hiding in the shadows. You can no longer get away with hiding in the shadows and settle for morphing into a false version of whom you were created to be. Your job is to shine. Your job is to be visible. Your job is to drink sweet nectar – enjoy life, find your mate – connect with like-minded butterflies to collaborate with, and to lay eggs – deposit the seeds of wisdom and knowledge that you have gathered along the journey.

A moth is notorious for impersonating other animals and insects. They can mimic a tarantula or a wasp as a way of self-preservation. Some moths even mimic bird droppings.[60] You are not a moth and have no business mimicking things that are unbecoming of whom you were created to be. You no longer need to disguise yourself as anything other than the most authentic version of yourself.

I see you. I see your butterfly. My sister, it is time to rise.

Summoned to Soar

As I write the final chapter of this book, I want to remind you, Amelia Earhart. Her skill played a big part in her ability to become the first woman to cross the Trans-Atlantic flying solo in an airplane, but it is said that it was her confidence that ultimately assisted her in accomplishing such a great feat. Confidence, to Amelia Earhart, was defined as the willingness to go after the impossible and the belief in herself that she could achieve it.[61] My prayer is that as you have read the pages of this book, you have said YES to YOUR impossible. I hope that you have said YES to locating, defining and designing the impossible that was deposited inside of your when you were in your mother's womb. Finally, it is my prayer that your belief in yourself explodes to new levels so that you can achieve your impossible.

How do you know when you are ready to fly? You will not compromise who you are. You choose not to betray yourself anymore. You know your purpose. You know how to posture yourself – perpendicular to the ground, standing erect so that your crown stays put. You can now ask for what you want with boldness. You have learned how to partner with the wind soar to new heights.

No matter what phase of life you are in now, rest assured that the season of *The Rise* is where the journey leads. God has not forgotten about you if you are in the phase of *The Ordinary*. He dropped the dreams of extraordinary down on the inside of you to compel you toward *The Rise*. God is not punishing you when you are wrapped up in the grace-lined, dark night of your soul – the belly of the cocoon – *The Becoming* phase of metamorphosis. You were not born to stay locked up inside of a cocoon. Your final destination is not even in *The Debut*. *The Debut* paves the way to *The Rise*. I am looking for a butterfly nation – a company of women who are committed to being the most authentic version of themselves and no longer morphing into a false version of whom they were created to be. This is your time to rise.

You are being summoned to spread your wings and soar.

Angela Aja

Scriptural Basis for Coaching and Transformation

The principles of coaching are seen all throughout the Bible and I believe there is a strong biblical basis that supports coaching as a means of renewing the mind and true transformation.

1. **The Power Transformation by the of the Renewing of the Mind**

Our Spirit is saved but our mind needs to be continually renewed.

> Romans 12:2 *"Do not **conform** to the pattern of this **world**, but be **transformed** by the **renewing** of your mind. Then you will be able to test and approve what God's will is—his good, pleasing and perfect will." NIV [emphasis added]*

"Conform" means to fashion one's mind and character.
"World" is a Greek word "*aion*" – it is in the noun and masculine form – it means "a space of time, a cycle of time". What was going on at that time? (Instability, weakness, impiety, wickedness, misery, same as today) So, do not be controlled by the

thoughts and pursuits of this present time. Do not be controlled by instability, weakness or misery.

"Transformed" is the Greek word "*metamorphoo*" which is where we get the word "metamorphosis". Metamorphosis means to make a complete change, as in going from a caterpillar to a butterfly. It is derived from two Greek words that mean "to change after being with" and "changing form in keeping with inner reality."

"*Renewing*" is the same word as "*transformed.*"

The Greek word for "*of your mind*" is a Greek word that means "reflective thinking."[62]

Do not fashion your mind and your character to the pattern or the design of this cycle of time that we are living in; instability, weakness, and misery. As you are with your own thoughts (awareness without judgment,) make a complete change in your reflective thinking so that your inner reality aligns with whom you were originally created to be. The result will be true outward transformation, just like a caterpillar transforms into a butterfly.

2. The Power of Stable Thinking

> James 1:8 "*A double minded man is unstable in all his ways.*" KJV

The word for "double-minded" in the Greek language means "*two souls;*" one who wavers.

"Unstable in all of his ways" means "*someone who disagrees with himself.*"[63]

This is not referring to a hypocrite, but someone who is fickle; without consistency.

The art of coaching is a discovery process of authentic thinking through high-quality questions and active listening which allows one to sort out their thoughts and feelings. It brings about stability and consistency as well as opening up opportunities for deliberate action.

3. **The Power of Positive Thinking**

Proverbs 23:7 "As a man thinks in his heart, so is he." NKJV

Your thoughts shape your actions. What you believe about yourself and about the world is mirrored back to you in real life. Coaching provides an opportunity to look at the results of your life as feedback without judgment and to decide which ways of thinking are supporting you or holding you back.

4. **The Power of a Vision**

*Proverbs 29:18 "Where there is no **vision**, the people perish: but he that keeps the law, happy is he." KJV [emphasis added]*

The NIV says, "Where there is no **revelation**, people cast off restraint; but blessed are the one who heeds wisdom's instruction." [emphasis added]

The word "vision" means "*divine communication*", literally "*mental sight.*"

The word "perish" means "*let go*" or "*dismiss.*"[64]

The vision constrains you to your mission and purpose. It holds you accountable to who you are, why you are here and what you are here to do. Your vision is the end result of living your mission and purpose. It is bigger than where you are at this moment. A commitment to your vision keeps you focused on where you are going so that what you want becomes bigger than your fears. It keeps you on track so that you do not dismiss the divine insight about your purpose.

Consider this...if you get in your car, put your seatbelt on, put the keys in the ignition, turn on the car and put the car in drive but you are looking at your belly button, how far will you get without a crash? The answer is-NOT VERY FAR! You move in the direction of your vision. What you look at is where you go. Vision is key to living a life of intentional impact.

Coaching offers a new perspective and assists you in gaining a clear mental sight about your present and future with a fresh outlook. If you take your eyes off of where you are going, you will become easily distracted and get "stuck in a rut."

5. The Power of Truth

> *Psalms 51:6, "Behold, You desire truth in the innermost being, And in the hidden part [of my heart] You will make me know wisdom."* AMP

The word "truth" means *"true* and *lasting."*[65] It has the idea of something that is *SURE, STABLE* and *RELIABLE*. It is consistent and dependable. The word "innermost parts" means *"the seat of faithfulness."*[66] Another word for faithfulness is authenticity.

Coaching digs down underneath the layers upon layers of masks that you pile on top of the truest essence of whom you were created to be. It gets underneath who you have become to unlock who you really are.

Mindsets, Patterns, and Behaviors

A dynamic, spiritual life is a life of consistently up-leveling your mindset. When you up-level your mindset, you create new patterns which in turn, create new behaviors.

Fear is a mindset. Faith is a mindset. Forgiveness is a mindset. Resentment is a mindset. Love is a mindset. Joy is a mindset.

> *Philippians 2:5 states, "Let this mind be in you which was also in Christ Jesus." KJV*

The meaning of "the mind" in Greek is "*to think.*"[67] Your job is to think as Christ thought. Further, it means that your inner perspective corresponds with your outer behavior.

What kind of mindset did Christ have? Christ was committed to the vision of his mission and purpose. He was committed to behaving in a way that corresponded with His inner beliefs about what He came to earth to do.

As a woman on her journey to *The Rise*, you now have an opportunity to do the same. Commit to the vision of your mission and purpose. Behave in a way that corresponds with your inner beliefs so that you can show up in the world fearlessly and make a bigger impact.

Angela Aja

Notes

1. Copyright Life Coach Hub Ltd, 2016 https://www.lifecoachhub.com/beginners-guide-to-life-coaching/history-of-life-coaching
2. https://icfhoustoncoaches.org/What_Coaching_Is_Not
3. https://www.merriam-webster.com/dictionary/transformation
4. https://www.amentsoc.org/insects/glossary/terms/incomplete-metamorphosis
5. Dictionary.com Unabridged Based on the Random House Unabridged Dictionary, © Random House, Inc. 2018
6. http://www.horseracinggold.com/Turn-Time.htm
7. https://www.lamaze.org/HealthyBirthPractices
8. https://sciencing.com/inchworm-life-cycle-6122809.html
9. https://www.merriam-webster.com/dictionary/disappointment
10. https://www.merriam-webster.com/dictionary/appointment
11. © 2019 Genius Media Group Inc. Gloria Gaynor, Artist, Love Tracks, Album, Freddie Perren and Dino Fekaris, Songwriters 1978
12. https://www.britannica.com/topic/Encarta Encarta Encyclopedia Britannica, Encyclopedia Britannica, Inc, Richard Pallardy, June 27, 2017
13. https://www.biblestudytools.com/dictionary/cave/
14. https://dwwork.wordpress.com/2012/08/27/he-had-been-in-the-tomb-four-days

15. Songwriters: Joel Houston / Matt Crocker / Salomon Lighthelm Oceans (Where Feet May Fail) lyrics © Songtrust Ave, Capitol Christian Music Group
16. https://www.scientificamerican.com/article/caterpillar-butterfly-metamorphosis-explainer/
17. https://www.merriam-webster.com/dictionary/calling
18. https://www.monarch-butterfly.com/monarch-butterflies-facts.html
19. https://bible.org/article/thirty-three-words-sin-new-testament-part-1
20. https://www.myjewishlearning.com/article/repentance/
21. https://www.blueletterbible.org/lang/lexicon/lexicon.cfm?t=kjv&strongs=g3341
22. https://www.merriam-webster.com/dictionary/become
23. https://www.merriam-webster.com/dictionary/selfish?utm_campaign=sd&utm_medium=serp&utm_source=jsonld
24. https://www.merriam-webster.com/dictionary/self-love
25. http://www.womenshealth.northwestern.edu/blog/memory-telephone-game
26. https://www.merriam-webster.com/dictionary/sorry
27. https://www.zmescience.com/ecology/animals-ecology/how-caterpillar-turn-butterfly-0534534/
28. https://www.sciencedirect.com/science/article/pii/0012160692900521
29. http://www.crivoice.org/WT-esther.html
30. https://www.christiantoday.com/article/3-ways-to-determine-if-youre-a-spiritual-eunuch/120704.htm
31. https://biblehub.com/topical/h/hegai.htm
32. Https://en.wikipedia.org/wiki/Myrrh
33. https://drericz.com/truth-about-gold-frankincense-and-myrrh/

34. http://www.wholemagazine.org/posts/olemagazine.org/2014/09/preparing-to-meet-your-king.html
35. https://www.google.com/search/debut
36. This Little Light of Mine Words and music by Harry Dixon Loes. Public Domain.
37. https://www.goodreads.com/author/quotes/17297.Marianne_Williamson
38. https://www.medicinenet.com/script/main/art.asp?articlekey=40205
39. https://www.reimangardens.com/butterfly/butterfliesmoths-spread-wings-emerging/
40. https://www.guideposts.org/inspiration/miracles/gods-grace/the-mysterious-power-of-stories
41. https://blog.bufferapp.com/science-of-storytelling-why-telling-a-story-is-the-most-powerful-way-to-activate-our-brains
42. https://www.mindblowing-facts.org/2013/01/a-butterfly-sees-you-through-their-12000-eyes/
43. https://sciencing.com/do-do-butterfly-crinkled-wings-8757961.html
44. https://www.reimangardens.com/butterfly/butterfliesmoths-spread-wings-emerging/
45. https://4cs.gia.edu/en-us/4cs-diamond-quality/
46. https://www.gia.edu/ruby
47. https://www.fourmine.com/education/gemstone-education/emerald-gemstone/emerald-meaning
48. https://www.jewelsforme.com/sapphire-meaning
49. www.townandcountrymag.com
50. http://science.sciencemag.org/content/294/5541/267.4
51. https://renner.org/have-you-noticed-people-god-called-to-help-you/

52. https://renner.org/have-you-noticed-people-god-called-to-help-you/
53. https://www.merriam-webster.com/dictionary/positioned
54. http://www.butterflyschool.org/new/behav.html
55. https://australianbutterflies.com/how-do-butterflies-fly/
56. https://australianbutterflies.com/how-do-butterflies-fly/
57. Dictionary.com Unabridged Based on the Random House Unabridged Dictionary, © Random House, Inc. 2018
58. Dictionary.com Unabridged Based on the Random House Unabridged Dictionary, © Random House, Inc. 2018
59. www.livescience.com
60. http://www.butterflyschool.org/student/butterfly.html
61. https://www.forbes.com/sites/jackzenger/2018/04/08/the-confidence-gap-in-men-and-women-why-it-matters-and-how-to-overcome-it/#47fd4f303bfa
62. © 2004 - 2018 by Bible Hub Copyright © 1987, 2011 by Helps Ministries, Inc.
63. © 2004 - 2018 by Bible Hub Copyright © 1987, 2011 by Helps Ministries, Inc.
64. © 2004 - 2018 by Bible Hub Copyright © 1987, 2011 by Helps Ministries, Inc.
65. NAS Exhaustive Concordance of the Bible with Hebrew-Aramaic and Greek Dictionaries Copyright © 1981, 1998 by The Lockman Foundation All rights reserved Lockman.org
66. © 2004 - 2018 by Bible Hub Copyright © 1987, 2011 by Helps Ministries, Inc.
67. © 2004 - 2018 by Bible Hub Copyright © 1987, 2011 by Helps Ministries, Inc.

Summoned To Soar

About the Author

Angela Aja is the founder and CEO of Confidence Builders, Inc. She is an ordained minister and certified life coach with over 30 years of experience mentoring and training leaders to shape impactful lives for themselves and their communities. Her mission is to empower women by helping them to align their life and career with their mission, vision, and purpose to create an existence of significance, fulfillment and true joy. Confident women showing up in the world fearlessly to make a bigger impact is the vision that compels her to continue to rise as she is summoned to soar.

As an author and speaker, Angela uses her transformative journey from tragedy to triumph, motivating women to move from inspiration to implementation for maximum impact. She uses her platform to walk women through a process of awakening to their authenticity, coming into alignment with their divine assignment and being activated into a life of extraordinary impact.

Angela is a trained chef from Le Cordon Bleu and a foodie through and through – a bon vivant, if you will. She is the mother to four children and self-proclaimed "Glammaw" who goes by the name of "Mammaw" to four precious grand-babies. Angela describes herself as a family fanatic and a midwestern girl with a Texas twist. Her two greatest passions are the transformation of food and the transformation of people.

To schedule your complimentary Clarity Call or speaking inquiries, visit http://www.confidencebuildersinc.com.

Summoned To Soar

Angela Aja

Made in the USA
Monee, IL
05 September 2022

12365741R00115